LIGHTWORKER RELATIONSHIPS

Creating Lasting and Healthy Bonds as an Empath

Sahvanna Arienta

Author of *Lightworker*

New Page Books
A division of The Career Press, Inc.
Pompton Plains, N.J.

LIGHTWORKER RELATIONSHIPS
EDITED BY KIRSTEN DALLEY
TYPESET BY EILEEN MUNSON
Original cover design by Jeff Piasky
Cover image by Detelina Petkova/shutterstock
Printed in the U.S.A.

To order this title, please call toll-free 1-800-CAREER-1 (NJ and Canada: 201-848-0310) to order using VISA or MasterCard, or for further information on books from Career Press.

The Career Press, Inc.
12 Parish Drive
Wayne, NJ 07470
www.careerpress.com
www.newpagebooks.com

Library of Congress Cataloging-in-Publication Data
Names: Arienta, Sahvanna, 1966-
Title: Lightworker relationships : creating lasting and healthy bonds as an empath / by Sahvanna Arienta.
Description: Wayne : Career Press, Inc., 2016. | Includes bibliographical references and index.
Identifiers: LCCN 2015038564| ISBN 9781632650252 (alk. paper) | ISBN
    9781632659736 (ebook : alk. paper)
Subjects: LCSH: Psychics. | Interpersonal relations--Miscellanea.
Classification: LCC BF1040 .A74 2016 | DDC 131--dc23
LC record available at http://lccn.loc.gov/2015038564

When a student is ready a teacher will appear.
—Tao saying

For my greatest teacher, my mother:
I was born ready.

*The weak fall, but the strong shall remain
and never go under!*
—Anne Frank

For my sister, my inspiration and a powerful
warrior of the light.

Contents

Introduction

I will start this book with good news: Lightworkers have come to earth to help heal the planet. Empathic, sensitive, unique souls, Lightworkers make great sacrifices to fulfill their divine mission and be of service to humanity. But there is some bad news, too: Lightworkers often forget that they have needs to be nurtured, too. Consequently they overlook their own need to be loved by others. When they forget this, they lose sight of their authentic self. As Lightworkers use their light energy to be of service, they give of themselves without limitations. Although they naturally harbor a great deal of light energy, it is not an endless resource but one that must be replenished constantly by accepting love and light energy in return. Often this light energy comes via loving and functional relationships. So it is essential that Lightworkers be able to take in light energy, in order to stay in balance and in alignment with their divine purpose. Without being able to receive, they quickly become depleted, and their energy moves into a very dark place, indeed.

In my practice most Lightworkers come to me about relationship issues, because it is so easy for them to become depleted in their interactions with others. They are constantly on a quest to "top off" the unconditional love energy that is within the heart chakra space, because this is the channel through which their healing gifts flow. (You will read all about chakras in the first chapter.) Love is what fuels their divine mission. Many experience difficulty in relationships because of their inherently generous nature. They are in a sense perfect targets for those who do not want to heal or be healed, but who only want to drain the vital energy of a Lightworker. Sadly, Lightworkers' need for love often causes them to stay in painful or dysfunctional relationships. They usually have no idea why they feel so used, so depleted, and, ultimately, so utterly abandoned by the very people to whom they have shown such unconditional love. This often sets off a vicious cycle, wherein the Lightworker's heart becomes wounded and, eventually, closes itself off, shutting down the Lightworker's healing gifts and leading him or her down a painful road of wounded emotions, toxic energy, and all the attendant complications therein. This puts the Lightworker into a dark cavern from which it is nearly impossible to extricate him- or herself.

Because you picked up this book, this probably sounds all too familiar to you. My goal in writing this book is to give you clarity and insight into the dynamics of how Lightworkers tend to function within relationships, and why their personal relationships seem to continuously put them in a dark place. The information in these pages is going to help you see yourself in a new "light," so to speak—not just as a Lightworker who is here to heal the planet, but as someone who can receive as well as give. The energy dynamics of your relationships are likely affecting you in ways that you may not understand or even consciously be able to process. You will learn how to be aware of these dynamics—these exchanges of energy between yourself and others—and how they affect your emotional well-being, your physical health, and, most importantly, your spirituality.

A Lightworker's unique sensitivities combined with his or her overall need to be of service can tend to interfere with personal relationships if these gifts are not harnessed or channeled in the proper way. We tend to attract wounded partners because we always want to follow that instinct to "fix" or heal others. Then we get caught up in a vicious cycle of repetitive negative behaviors in a constant quest to heal our own selves in the aftermath. Many

Lightworkers find themselves alone and feeling unwanted because they continuously attract the type of partner whose energy is lacking or in distress. These types of partners simply cannot give the type of love the Lightworker needs or is worthy of. Both healer and wounded are like moths to a flame for each other, energetic magnets, if you will, with the Lightworker wanting nothing more than to heal, and the wounded person obsessively seeking that powerful light energy to *be* healed. What you will soon discover is that there is the time and place for the Lightworker to heal. Learning to compartmentalize these urges and make the proper space in your life for your gifts will help you develop equitable and balanced personal relationships. Lightworker, you were put here on this earth not only to heal but to live a joyful life. You deserve nothing less!

So how can we attract healthy relationships, rather than these unhealthy interactions with others that leave us wounded and shut down? We will discuss the different ways Lightworkers attract wounded partners, the traps we fall into, the roles we play, and how the cycles of dysfunction become a part of our makeup. Once we find ourselves in these painful cycles and allow them to continue, they can dominate our lives. With our great power to heal also comes great vulnerability. I will show you how to avoid the pitfalls that come along with your Lightworker gifts. As well, learning about ourselves and what we truly want will help us attract what we authentically desire. The universe in its simplicity brings you exactly what you ask for, which at times can be quite a shock! Just because you are a Lightworker doesn't mean you are always aware of what you are asking of the universe. Learning to discern the difference between what you truly desire out of a relationship and what you're actually asking for—what you're attracting—is so important.

But how do we put our real desire for love and relationship out into the universe in such a way that it is returned to us in a way that fulfills our need to love and be loved as a spirit, not just a healer? Here we begin to see the paradoxical nature of the Lightworker's higher calling: How does the Lightworker, a consummate giver, also learn to accept love in return? This is a question we will explore, and as we begin to love and understand our authentic selves, we can then ask the universe for that perfect partner to share our journey with.

This book is about love, relationships, and the desires of our hearts, and how we navigate it all as Lightworkers. But it is also about knowing ourselves and identifying what we need, as empathic and highly sensitive souls, to be fulfilled, how to ask for it, and how to actually allow ourselves to receive it freely and with joy.

Are you ready? Let's begin!

(Author's note: All names and identifying details in this book have been changed to protect privacy.)

PART I

Ambassadors From Heaven

As you probably already know, being a Lightworker is not just a gift, but a calling. This calling is something you have been chosen for and have chosen to fulfill. Before Lightworkers come to earth to live life in their physical body, they make a sacred agreement with their source creator to leave the higher planes of existence and come to earth as healers. These souls must reach a particular stage of enlightenment before they can incarnate here on earth and start their mission. Their mission is, always, to bring healing energy to the planet in some way, shape, or form. As a Lightworker yourself, you probably feel perpetually driven to help, to be of service, to spread your light energy. Lightworkers are heaven's ambassadors on earth, different from what we know as angels but still from a higher place. These ambassadors make the ultimate sacrifice to come to earth—a harsh and sometimes cruel place—and many times these sensitive souls suffer much confusion and despair before they awaken to who they really are. Once they realize their purpose and are set on a course to complete their mission, they can find a wonderful balance between humanity and spirituality. This place of balance is not easy to find, however. Lightworkers are truly heart-centered beings, meaning that all they do is powered by the love energy that comes through the heart chakra, right in the center of the chest, the center of your being. Lightworkers draw upon and channel this love energy from the highest source of all, God.

To truly appreciate yourself and your gifts, you must first understand that your true essence is energetic, or nonphysical. This energy you are made of is transformed into a physical manifestation (that is, your human form) and it forms everything you do and all you experience, including your relationships. Your physical body is just a temporary home for your spirit and the vehicle for your spirit to complete your work here on earth. The sensitive and distinctly complex soul of a Lightworker is unique and has specific needs and requirements to keep this energy (your spirit) healthy and vital.

The Chakras

Within your spiritual body are seven conduits that channel your energy and keep it moving in an orderly fashion. These channels are called *chakras*, which is a Sanskrit word for "wheel." The seven chakras are energy centers and conduits through which energy flows. As their name implies, they move and rotate universal energy through our physical body and hence are very important for our spiritual and physical well-being. Here is a brief overview of the seven chakras and their placements, physical associations and purposes.

+ **The first chakra,** located at the base of the spine, is called the root chakra. It is associated with the Earth plane and all things material. Our sense of security as well as our fears are stored here, as it keeps us grounded in the earth plane.

+ **The second chakra,** also known as the sacral chakra, is located just below the navel, and is associated with sexuality and self-esteem. This is where both the masculine and the feminine energies are stored and merge together.

+ **The third chakra** is located in the solar plexus and is essentially the will center. This is the place from which our will moves out into

the world in order to manifest those things
we are trying to create in our lives.

+ **The fourth chakra** is located at the heart
  and is related to love. This is where the love
  energy of the universe cycles through us.
  Lightworkers channel *all* their healing powers through this sacred conduit.

+ **The fifth chakra** is located at the throat, and
  is our channel for communication and the
  voice. Communicating ideas, concepts, and
  emotions and speaking for your authentic
  self comes via this chakra.

+ **The sixth chakra** is located at the position of
  the third eye, and is related to sight, insight,
  and time. This chakra is the seat of intuition
  and psychic abilities.

+ **The seventh chakra,** or the crown chakra,
  is located at the top of the head and is the
  point of connection to our source creator.
  Divine information comes via this chakra.

We will discuss each chakra and the part the
chakras play in relationships later. For now, we will
begin by focusing on the one that is most sacred to
the Lightworker: the fourth chakra, or heart chakra.

The heart chakra

Because Lightworkers heal through the power
of love, the heart chakra is their most sacred energy
space. Many Lightworkers guard this space fierce-
ly because it acts as the conduit for their healing

gifts and the place from which they move out and do their work here on earth. Guarding it too closely can be a double-edged sword, however, because this chakra is also their means of connecting with other people. After all, all Lightworkers are human and need to have their emotional needs fulfilled, just as all other people do, in order to maintain the optimal balance of body, mind, and spirit. When the human needs are not met, their energetic side (which channels love through the fourth, or heart, chakra) is weakened, and its source of connection to others begins to close off. This can be quite the conundrum for a Lightworker, because the work they have come here to complete on a spiritual level must engage that very same conduit that is used to foster their connection with others and satisfy their need to be loved. What is a Lightworker to do?

What's Love Got to Do With It?

The healing energy of love is where all the Lightworker's healing gifts come from. Love energy comes in many forms, shapes, and sizes. Sometimes a Lightworker's love of art and music brings beauty to the world, whereas another Lightworker can heal humanity simply by helping the needy. There are many ways the healing power of the love energy can be used to complete the Lightworker's mission. The primary area in which love energy tends to create difficulties in a Lightworker's life is in personal relationships. It is true that each Lightworker has a need to embrace a higher purpose and has come to earth on a sacred mission, but does this sacred mission have to come at the expense of true happiness for the Lightworker? Many times as a Lightworker you may forget that you are entitled to receive love and feel nurtured in return. In fact, loving and being loved—this mutual energetic exchange—are essential to completing your mission! A Lightworker cannot fulfill his or her sacred purpose without receiving love (light energy) in return. The energy exchange keeps an even, balanced ebb and flow of healthy fluidity constantly channeling through the love conduit, the heart chakra.

Sensitive Lightworkers can become so consumed by empathic emotions, energetic transmissions from others, and their innate need to be of service, that they tend to overlook what is essential to their work: keeping their heart chakra open and flowing with perpetually renewed love energy. Without this healthy equilibrium, light energy is depleted, and toxic energy is in overload. When this happens, the Lightworker starts to shut down, and the heart chakra becomes hardened and closed off. Simply put, the heart chakra slams shut to protect itself. When the heart chakra goes into "lockdown" mode, it is impossible to accept love from others. It also blocks your ability to share the healing gifts you came to earth to share. When the Lightworker becomes overwhelmed with toxic energy, the human ego (or conscious mind) goes on a mad dash to seek out light energy sources, either in safe places that bring no spiritual growth, or, worse, in outright dangerous places. Many times such Lightworkers will find themselves trapped in unhappy relationships in which their authentic self becomes bogged down and buried with layer upon layer of darkness. This mad dash usually manifests in the form of multiple dysfunctional relationships, destructive behavioral patterns, and, sometimes, vicious cycles of abuse. Other Lightworkers take the safer route and isolate themselves entirely. Some find connection with animals—a safe source of love but one that cannot fulfill the need for human connection. In sum, any time love energy is not processed properly, the heart chakra will go into this "lockdown" mode, which in turn will prevent any type of personal relationship from developing in a healthy way.

When you get to a place where all you can do is give but never receive, all you're doing is continually putting out love energy, further depleting your light energy, and blocking your healing gifts. When a Lightworker is blocked and trapped in a dysfunctional relationship or in a state of isolation, her feelings of self-worth diminish; she begins to interpret this feeling as proof that she is incapable of loving or of being loved. This puts her in the precarious and vulnerable situation of being abused or manipulated by others who are prone to exploit someone who is so susceptible. Then the Lightworker will actually feel guilty for being abused, because she "brought it on herself." Lightworkers take on the blame or responsibility for the abuse because their need to heal and be of service is not being fulfilled. Lightworkers will sacrifice their own wellbeing without a thought in order to please everyone and keep the peace.

Many times these beautiful, gentle souls have little awareness of how to help themselves in these situations because their inner calling to help others takes precedence over everything else. This is by no means a personality defect, and it doesn't mean you are weak or somehow defective. Quite the opposite! It just means you need to develop an awareness of your sacred role and how it factors into your total being, which includes both the human and the spiritual side.

An Energetic Sponge

Many Lightworkers feel isolated and out of sync with others and when it comes to developing healthy personal relationships; in this sense their own gifts actually become a hindrance. Empathy is a powerful force for the Lightworker. Although it is a healing gift at times it can wreak havoc in your personal life if you let it. The empathetic Lightworker will actually attract and be attracted to the wounded. Why would someone want to attract a wounded partner? Because of an inner need to heal humanity, which, again, comes from a place not of this earth. Lightworkers come from a higher place where pain and suffering do not exist. The earth plane is heavy with dark energy and needs these soldiers of the light to keep it in balance. Yes, you have a sacred purpose to heal the wounded, but without proper awareness you will actually take on the wounds as your own burden and try to shoulder the pain yourself. This is a mistake. It takes a lot of awareness to understand that these feelings of pain and energetic sicknesses are not yours, but belong to someone else. When you finally do recognize that you are acting as an energetic sponge, you can "wring out" all these emotions that you have absorbed unadvisedly and begin the process of cleansing.

Returning to Self-Love

The loss of self-esteem and self-worth and subsequent heartache that comes with these relationships is usually difficult to recover from for the Lightworker. Through it all they lose sight of what is authentically their own energy. Being so sensitive and empathic to everyone and everything around you can also open up an overwhelming flood of emotions, which may in turn put you in a downward spiral of self-loathing and low self-esteem. Particularly in personal relationships, your human need for validation is also involved. So this not only becomes a spiritual pain, but your humanity will also suffer. Spirits need no validation, but the human counterpart we all identify with needs the human connection to thrive. We see this in infants whose mothers do not bond with them properly. The babies fail to thrive properly and their development is stunted. Human connection is essential in everyone's incarnation.

Healing practices to release this toxic energy and reopen your heart chakra will be discussed later, but it is a long and quite challenging process returning to that original state of self-love that you came to earth with. Uncovering the layers and layers of toxic energy that have caused heart chakra "lockdown" can be laborious and painful. However, doing the hard work of sorting out our energy and maintaining proper balance in our entire chakra system is needed to maintain spiritual and physical well-being. Many times this will mean excavating painful memories or experiences that you'd probably prefer to keep buried. But in order to cleanse and open up this sacred channel, the heart, the pain *must* be brought to the surface, embraced, and then processed to make room for light energy. Like peeling away the layers of an onion, you're bound to shed some tears in the process. However, as you begin to get closer and closer to your true core, you will get to the place of self-love and authenticity that will enable you to open up and receive love from others in a healthy, constructive way. For those who have been trapped in cycles of unhealthy relationships and are locked down with toxic energy, it is important to begin as soon as possible. Sadly, rehabilitation may take several years or even decades without the proper awareness and guidance. If you are reading this and feel you have come to this unfortunate place, not to worry: We will discuss many ways to uncover the love in your heart and open you up once again.

If you constantly find yourself in toxic relationships, it's likely that you are attracting one or more of the following types:

✦ Emotionally unavailable.

✦ Physically unavailable (for example married or otherwise partnered, geographically undesirable).

✦ Addict.

✦ Narcissist.

✦ Passive aggressive.

✦ Controller.

✦ Perfectionist.

✦ Manipulator.

✦ Codependent.

✦ Commitment phobic.

✦ Abusive, emotionally or physically.

✦ Afraid of intimacy.

✦ Overly needy.

✦ Overly jealous.

If you feel you have been attracting partners with these traits, you may be a Lightworker in need of a new perspective on relationships and, most of all, on your authentic self. Read on and we will discuss how you can be safe from the vulnerable position of being in the "lockdown" mode that comes with loving and coexisting with these types. In the next chapters we will discuss how to avoid attracting or being attracted to these types of people and how to gain mastery of our Lightworker role and achieve happiness as a human being.

CHAPTER 2

Examining Our Most Sacred Space

Lightworkers come to earth with an endless source of light energy to complete their healing mission. This energy comes from the most powerful source in the universe, a source so profound and expansive that it is impossible to describe with mere words. It is the source of everything that ever was or ever shall be, our creator. It is that constant, pulsating vibration that resonates through every form of life on the planet. Even things we don't consider to be alive, such as stars, rainbows, the ocean, and even a gentle breeze, are all fueled by this powerful energy. It is comprised of one element only: unconditional love. Lightworkers help to heal the planet by using the heart chakra as the conduit of this ultimate love source, the highest vibratory energy there is. The love energy heals, regenerates, and balances the energy of the entire planet and everything in it. The ability to feel compassion, sympathy, and gratitude as well as to heal is all channeled through this sacred conduit, the heart chakra. It is also the Lightworker's main source of connection to others.

How Do We Become Blocked?

As I already mentioned, the reason Lightworkers come to earth is to heal by using their enormous power. If the channel or conduit for this power is blocked for any reason, the Lightworker's power to heal becomes blocked, as well. Primarily these blocks occur through harboring toxic energy rather than "processing it through" properly. Sensitive and empathetic Lightworkers, mistakenly thinking they are being of service, often take on the pain and toxic energy of others and hold it for them. This is not healing; rather, it is enabling others to remain stuck in their pain and not heal for themselves. So the other person never grows or gets any better, and the whole process becomes counterproductive and even harmful to both people. Lightworkers in such a position, those who are not serving their purpose, often become lost in feelings of worthlessness and

despair. They feel misplaced, depressed, and useless, unable to do their job. If you are a Lightworker
and you do not protect your healing capacities, they
will quickly shut down, and you mission will never
be completed. For Lightworkers, living a heart-centered life—focusing one's energy on loving compassion—is the most important practice in keeping
them happy and vital.

A Purpose-Driven Life

If you identify with the Lightworker spirit, your
divine mission is to achieve mastery of your role,
which is healing and restoring balance to a planet
that is overcome with darkness. Lightworkers use
this energy in a way that may or may not be obvious
to others around them. Some heal the sick, some
create uplifting works of art, and others may simply have a presence or way about them that attracts
others. No matter what your occupation, lifestyle, or
ideals, this light energy will emanate from you without your ever having to say a word. People will naturally be drawn to your light, that "x-factor" that others cannot name or fully describe. For this reason,
a Lightworker is almost always the one the new kid
at school approaches for support, or the colleague
at work whom the new gal comes to for guidance.
The reasons for this are hard to explain. Maybe the
empathy Lightworkers embody gives them an air
of sympathy. Or maybe it's that the love emanating
from Lightworkers just makes them seem more ap-
proachable to others. Regardless, they always seem

to be beacons for the lost and the lonely. They always tend to be the defenders of the underdogs, the voice for those who have none.

Does this sound like you? Whether your light is a steady, subtle glow or a glaring spotlight, it doesn't matter—this irresistible quality will still make people stand up and take notice. Not only people, but animals, as well. My husband always likes to joke about how every stray cat or dog shows up at our doorstep! It's as though they know they will be safe, taken care of, and nurtured. (It doesn't end with stray cats and dogs, either—once we even had a chicken show up at our door! Very unusual for a family who doesn't live near any farms or barnyards.) The point is, if you're a Lightworker, you will attract all types, particularly those who are needy and in pain. This is why you need to set the boundaries and balance your spirit with your humanity.

Speaking of humanity...

There is a very good reason why people (and animals) to come to you: They are following the powerful energy of love. All living creatures can sense a healing presence, and they always desire to be near that energy, especially if they lack it. This may sound like a great way to be popular, but it actually becomes very draining and tiresome if you do not set boundaries. Consider whether you agree with any of the following statements:

+ In my relationships, it's always what the other person wants.

+ My friends have so many personal problems.

+ My husband/wife/partner doesn't appreciate all I do.

+ My family doesn't care how I feel.

+ My friends always want my advice but they never follow it.

+ I don't feel valued by my partner.

+ When I try to voice my feelings no one listens, so I just don't bother anymore.

+ I am usually the one who carries the burdens of my family.

+ I have a hard time saying no.

+ I consider myself a caretaker.

+ I could have been [insert your life's dream] if I didn't have to care for [needy person].

+ My partner/spouse is addicted and I need to help him or her to save our relationship.

+ I feel invisible except when someone wants something from me.

These statements tell you that your human self is suffering. Your experience here on earth is quite the lesson in balance. Both your spiritual self and your human self must achieve a healthy balance, with both being satisfied. If you feel that you are always being taken advantage of in personal relationships, it could mean that you are valorizing—giving preference to—your spiritual higher calling over your human interactions. But take heart: You can learn to separate the two and achieve a healthy balance so that all aspects of yourself are addressed and satisfied.

Wounds and Trauma

There are many reasons people lack light energy. Perhaps they have been wounded or traumatized and are seeking the unconditional love-energy you naturally exude. Some of these people are other Lightworkers who have not managed their energy properly and who are seeking out someone else's energy from which to draw. Or, perhaps they are simply people who have an emotional void to fill. Although this may sound a bit sinister, with all the connotations of vampires and feeding off the energy of others, but most of the time these are just lost souls in need of healing. It's important to know that being an authentic spiritual healer will a times present a risk your own human happiness.

All seven chakras described earlier are important and serve a purpose, but the heart chakra is *the* Lightworker's place of connection to others. The abundance of light energy within the heart chakra means that Lightworkers are especially sensitive to their feelings of connectedness in relationships. Their giving nature makes them want to direct more and more of this sacred energy into someone, just as if the other person were a target to hit, for their healing. Such targets can be romantic partners, friends, or just people whose personal happiness is closely tied to that of the Lightworker. As I mentioned, when the light or love energy is either drained or rejected to its limit, and the Lightworker is unable to take in any new healthy energy, the heart chakra can close up and become blocked. A wounded or depleted heart chakra will eventually tire and close down, thus cutting off the connection to others as well as to the Lightworker's own ability to conduct his or her light work. This in turn creates a vicious cycle: You begin to feel sad, isolated, and unloved because your lifeline has been blocked off. Picture a garden hose. When there is a kink in the hose, the water cannot flow through freely. It is blocked and cannot serve the purpose it was made for—to water flowers so they can bloom. The kink in the hose renders it temporarily useless. Same goes for the Lightworker whose life and love channel has been blocked. Now imagine this magnificently complex and sensitive being, sent from a place of pure love, unable to use his gifts to help others. He begins to feel useless. Then, he believes that he *is* useless. Eventually he will be literally unable to engage in a healthy relationship. He is blocked.

There are many reasons a Lightworker will close off her heart chakra, and there are as many ways to go about doing it. It usually occurs from trauma. After a trauma, toxic energy becomes trapped in a blocked heart chakra. Eventually this energy will manifest physically, often as an illness, which is yet another reason to keep your sacred conduit open, healthy, and flowing with clean, healthy love energy! This closing off of the heart chakra can happen at any age and at any time. Sometimes children will shut it down when they are feeling unloved or not properly nurtured by their parents. Young teens can be so traumatized by a failed first love that they close up and never experience the exhilaration that a first love can bring again. Likewise, an adult can experience a significant loss or hurt and close up shop for good. Remember: Lightworkers are acutely sensitive beings, so it may not take much for them to shut down.

The answer to not shutting down starts with *awareness*. If you're a parent dealing with a sensitive child, you must choose your words carefully. If you have a sensitive partner, be aware of his or her unique sensitivities. It's all about being aware of how to keep the heart chakra healthy and open in others. Loss and trauma happen to all of us; they are part of the physical experience. But disappointments and pain are not meant to shut down our love for others; they are meant to strengthen our resolve and prepare us for what is to come. Disappointments are simply a redirection onto a new path. We cannot simply close off our love for others because we have been in pain, because when we do this, we literally close off our love for our own self. You have been put here on earth with all the resources you need to carry out your life's plan. As a Lightworker you may be sensitive, but you are also among the mightiest warriors on the planet.

Lightworkers who experience trauma or pain, particularly in relationships, will likely go into protection mode. It's like battening down the hatches of a ship to prepare for the next storm. This presents a number of problems, which then compound into even more problems, creating the cycle spiraling into an abyss of darkness. Even though closing off your heart chakra cuts off your healthy connection to others, your human ego still urges you to seek out some kind of connection, *any* connection, even if it's not good for you. Usually this will send you on a misguided search for companionship that ends in dysfunctional or codependent relationships, sometimes even with disastrous results. Understanding how a Lightworker can keep his or her channel for love open and free from toxic energy is the key to happiness and loving connections with others. Protecting your most sacred conduit should be your first priority, because keeping the love energy flowing will have a positive effect on every aspect of your life. We will discuss ways to reopen your heart chakra and welcome people in who will bring you joy and happiness.

Have you battened down your hatches?

Look at the following list and see how many you can answer yes to. If you answer yes to a majority of them, you may be in danger of closing off your channel of love and light, or it may already be closed.

+ Do you find it difficult to let go of the past?
+ Do you have trouble forgiving others?
+ Do you consider yourself a victim of others' self-serving behavior?

✦ Do you find yourself avoiding the company of friends or loved ones?

✦ Do you feel isolated even when you are in the company of others?

✦ Do you feel you suffer from fear of commitment?

✦ Do you often engage in physical intimacy and later regret it?

✦ Do you refuse to forgive yourself for your past mistakes?

✦ Are you a workaholic or do you partake in other activities (exercising, eating, playing video games, drinking) in excess?

✦ Do you fear revealing your vulnerability even in safe, loving interactions?

✦ Do you have way too many pets, and although you love them, you know you have too many?

✦ Do you suffer from cardiovascular issues (high or low blood pressure, heart palpitations, etc.)?

✦ Do you fear rejection to the extent that it stops you from pursuing what you want?

✦ Do you use online dating sites or find that most of your interactions are online?

✦ Do you find yourself stuck in unhealthy relationship patterns?

✦ Are most of the people you attract addicted, wounded, or damaged in some way?

✦ Do you attract partners who are married, attached, or emotionally or geographically unavailable?

If you answered yes to many or most of these questions, you may have already shut down your heart chakra. This means you are no longer able to accept healthy love energy. Continuously feeling unhappy or taken advantage of is a clear sign you are not receiving healthy love energy from people in your life. This also means that you have most likely been holding on to toxic energy in your heart. When you cannot find happiness in love, it is probably because you have not processed the pain from your past. This means it is time to embark on a healing journey yourself. This will be a journey *back* to love and a journey *toward* self-discovery. As you begin to open your heart and restore your ability to connect to the authentic love source that is so deeply buried, you will discover that you can receive the most profound love you could ever imagine, not for others but also for yourself.

CHAPTER 3

Nurturing Both the Spirit and the Human Identity

There are many books and teachings about nurturing the spirit, a process that is essential to every Lightworker and, indeed, every human being on the planet. However, many New Age teachings forget to mention that the human factor is a huge part of the entire spiritual experience. Yes, the material and physical aspects of your incarnation are temporary factors; they are transient situations, not eternal like your spirit. But the physical body and the humanness of this earthly experience

are the springboards for a healthy and soaring spirit as well as the vehicle through which you achieve
mastery of your role.

As healers, sensitives, and empaths we sometimes overlook the fact that we are all too human,
as well. When we do this, the balance of human and
spirit is thrown off kilter. The intrinsic need to be
of service or to take an active part in the healing of
the planet can sometimes overtake the more pro-
saic needs of our human ego. All people need physical connection; we need human interaction on both
a physical and emotional level. For example, when
soulmates meet, the level of intensity the connection
brings is magical, but if the physical situation is not
conducive to the two souls progressing together in
the current lifetime, it can present many obstacles
to the connection. I have heard many of my clients
say they connected with their soulmate but it didn't
work out. How is this possible? Well, if we lived in
only a spiritual world, there would be no impedi-
ments, and soulmates could ride off into the sunset.
But we live in a material world, and, well, life gets
in the way. This doesn't mean that the soulmates
may not pick up with each other in another lifetime
when circumstances are more conducive, but in this
lifetime, if it's nothing but an uphill battle, perhaps
it's best to take what joy you gathered and move on,
"until we meet again."

So this shows us that Lightworkers are human,
too, and often have all-too-human egos, needs, and
sometimes self-serving desires. This is not contrary
to your authentic nature, nor is it a negative or dark

thing; rather, this is a side of yourself you must learn to embrace. Loving and accepting every part of yourself—spirit, mind, *and* body—is the way a Lightworker remains balanced and on course.

Human Adaptation and Spiritual Balance

In order to survive here in human form, we Lightworkers must learn to adapt to our mortal state. Lightworkers who deny this part of themselves find themselves feeling out of sync, isolated, and home-sick for the higher planes of their true home. This homesickness can last your entire life if you cannot adapt as a human. You were put here to use your human form to complete your work, and in order to do this you must *honor and value your human iden-tity*. People have needs that are actually encoded in their DNA. These codes are just as important to a Lightworker on a mission as the energetic "codes" that guide the Lightworker to mastery. Being human is not a shameful event; it is an honor to be chosen to come here and take on the challenge of helping to heal the planet. Think of your physical identity as the noble counterpart to your Lightworker soul, your partner-in-crime and the coauthor of the book of your life.

Another way to honor your mortality and nur-ture its well-being is by seeking out what it needs to thrive. The spirit's human counterpart picks up emotional baggage through the human experience. Because spirit and human identity must coexist, the human baggage is shared equally with the spiritual counterpart. The idea here is to understand that as we live our mortal life, we cannot neglect our human needs and allow ourselves to fall into the default mode of functioning only on a spiritual level. This is where Lightworkers can start to experience human dis-ease. The Lightworker spirit's innate need to always give wages an inner battle with the human ego that clamors to receive.

Coupling and romance are all around us. Genetically we are designed for this. We are drawn to finding a partner because, biologically speaking, we are programmed to. The human race needs to continue, so humans have a need to procreate. Our bodies also thrive on human contact and touch, so the desire to couple is not only for the purpose of procreation; human touch is needed to survive and thrive. Our five senses are designed to be stimulated by the environment we inhabit as well as those who share that space with us, to help keep us vital. So this need for human connection is a biological imperative that supports our vitality.

That being said, we need to separate the biological urge from the need for spiritual connection. Spiritual love is energetic in nature, whereas human love is experiential. Human experience and connection bring along with them all kinds of material attachments. For example, many people associate loss with the human love experience. This is why it summons up such fear in many people. A breakup is a loss, a death is a loss, family estrangement is a loss. Loss cannot occur on a spiritual level, because energy never dies; it only transforms. You can never lose your spirit or the spiritual connection to another. So here we learn the difference between what is eternal (spirit) and what is temporary (mortality). Spiritually the energetic love you feel for another person is not attached to anything that can be lost, so there should be no fear of loss. This puts a very different spin on love, doesn't it? We no longer feel ownership or entitlement to another person's human life or life choices. As well, this releases the fears of abandonment and the pain associated when someone detaches from you (for example, during a breakup).

Still the human side in us will latch onto this pain because it is always fearful of losing the physical aspect of the human love experience. This can hardly be helped, but if we can balance the need for the human experience with our spiritual energy (our spiritual connection being eternal), this will allow us to look at relationships much differently. With the realization that simply being human promotes a fear of loss, we can chose to look at love on a spiritual level that is, perhaps for the first time, free from fear.

Attracting the Wounded

When our healing role as a Lightworker begins to interfere with our human experience, we tend to enter into relationships that are imbalanced and unhealthy. Usually when we inadvertently get into a relationship in "full Lightworker mode," we tend to attract (or even seek out, which we will discuss later) wounded partners or those who are out to drain our energy. The Lightworker will pour out his love energy, and his partner will willingly accept it, and accept it, and accept it. Soon the Lightworker becomes depleted. Problems arise when the Lightworker's partner becomes so used to being a "taker" that she has essentially been trained not to give. As the Lightworker's light is drained away, the human resentment sets in. Know that this is counterproductive to your role, because by doing all the heavy lifting for your partner, you are blocking his or her ability to heal. The Lightworker and the wounded partner create a perfect symbiosis of a codependent relationship. The Lightworker needs to feel that he is of service, and the walking wounded does not want to address her own pain. Forgetting his own humanity, the empathetic Lightworker begins to feel neglected, taken advantage of, and manipulated, and ultimately begins to resent the partner. Then the vicious cycle repeats itself over and over again.

Another relationship dynamic occurs when the Lightworker constantly seeks out wounded partners in order to satisfy her need, her higher calling, to heal. Some Lightworkers don't realize they are actively seeking out wounded partners. Ultimately they find themselves unhappy and feeling used in their relationships, but they consistently fail to recognize that they call in these wounded partners. I often wonder why women who are otherwise energetic, goal-orientated, and well-rounded find themselves in relationships with men who are happy to take from them, but who cannot seem to give. Oftentimes these are addicted or dysfunctional men who cannot hold gainful employment because of personality disorders or other long-standing issues. These are the men who cannot commit or men who have a long list of shredded relationships in their wake. When I counsel these wonderful women, I often find they have an inner calling to be of service. But they are misguided in their efforts. The need to heal and be of service is a natural inclination for them, but they are attaching it to their human experience and then wondering where they went wrong.

Reassigning Your Role

My client Judith (not her real name) was always coming to me with relationship issues. She never felt validated in her relationships, and her self-worth was plummeting with each new attempt to couple with a male. Every man she was attracted to made a wonderful impression at the beginning. He was her dream man, she was certain he was "the one," and of course the connection was so powerful. I started to see a pattern, though, as each relationship began like a romance novel and then rapidly deteriorated into what better resembled a horror story. The men who were described as Mr. Wonderful soon were discovered to be addicts, abusers, control freaks—you name it. Judith would jump in quickly and inadvertently engage a man in her Lightworker capacity, but her human side was blind to the dangers. She would begin to feel unhappy and taken advantage of, and eventually she would discover that he was not the standup guy she thought he was at the beginning. Then she would begin the process of dealing with the pain and agony of being taken advantage of and used all over again.

Judith identified herself as a healer and Lightworker, but in our sessions, as we began to dig deeper and deeper into Judith's energy and deep within her heart chakra, I saw that she was harboring a toxic need for self-validation through relationships. Spirit showed me a child who yearned for the love and attention of her father, a man she idolized and who was also a functioning alcoholic. Although her father had been present in the home, he always favored her brother, who played football and who was his pride and joy. Judith felt cast aside, and this feeling stayed with her into her adult life. Judith carried this need for validation all her life, and it interfered with her ability to connect to men and relationships.

Because her father was in the grips of an addiction, Judith was also compelled to heal and "fix" others. As a sensitive child Judith picked up on her father's issues quite easily. So in her adult relationships with men, she was searching out a source of validation that she lacked as a child. Her Lightworker side was seeking out wounded partners in an effort to "fix." What was the solution? She needed to work through her pain to get to the place of knowing that only *she* could fill her inner void. She also needed to understand and accept that the wounded partners she was attracting didn't *want* to be healed. We worked together to dig deep and cleanse all the toxic energy she was holding in her heart chakra and began exercises in self-love and validation. Eventually her heart chakra opened up and the toxic energy was released, but it didn't happen overnight.

Judith's healing process was a journey, but in the end it brought her to a place of self-acceptance and recognition of the fact that she was not only attracting wounded partners, but she was *attracted to* wounded partners, too. She needed to change her role in her romantic relationships, and find the balance and middle ground to satisfy herself both spiritually and on a human level. She took up the practice of Reiki and began to work on self-love. Eventually she felt better-rounded spiritually and more completely grounded in her humanity, in a place where she was ready to find love.

If you're a Lightworker, whether you're male or female, there's a good chance you've been putting out energetic signals that attract the wounded, just as Judith was. Whether these signals are subtle or obvious, you're doing it naturally and without even thinking about it because it's all part of the healing energy that you harbor within you.

It all comes down to balance

In the end it is all about balance and accepting all the parts of ourselves. Yes, Lightworkers are healers and come to this planet to be of assistance, but they also have their own human agendas. It can be difficult to find your level in the "middle zone" and satisfy both your need to spread love and your need to be loved, especially if you have been wounded by an endless cycle of dysfunctional relationships. Here are some practical suggestions for how you can keep your human side grounded and stable while satisfying spirit:

✦ If someone is constantly telling you their problems and never asks about yours, step back from them for a while.

✦ If you feel drained, take a walk outdoors and connect with the energy of nature and the material world.

✦ If you feel your family does not honor your life dreams, do something for yourself that validates your gifts.

✦ Take good care of your physical body: Get proper exercise, eat right, etc.

✦ Do not engage in physical intimacy unless you feel loved and valued.

✦ Stay away from too much social networking or a lot of online interaction; you need face-to-face interaction.

✦ Wear colors or clothing that makes you feel radiant and physically attractive. Avoid baggy or unflattering clothing. Think of yourself as a magnificent work or art, which always requires an exquisite frame. Honor your body.

+ Do not indulge in excessive drugs or alcohol to derive courage to socialize; you're perfectly fine without them.

+ Always remember that we all have human flaws. They are what make us all unique, and diversity is attractive and exciting!

+ Love yourself the way you are. If you were meant to be taller, you would be. If you were meant to have perfect teeth, you would have perfect teeth. If it were necessary for you to have certain physical characteristics, you would have them. Remember that you are equipped with everything you need to fulfill your life's work.

PART II

CHAPTER 4

Human Connection and Working Through Pain

When we enter this lifetime we make a sacred commitment to bring light energy to the planet through our Lightwork. Lightwork can be practiced in many different ways. We don't necessarily need to show off or broadcast our intentions. We can be Lightworkers simply by how we choose to live in our human capacity. For many this involves being kind and forgiving, living in gratitude, having faith in the creator, and seeing one's life from a joyous perspective. All these feelings or actions bring more light energy to the planet. Being a Lightworker is all about living your purpose and being content with and within your humanity. This is why our human side needs to be connected to the earth and to others who are here living their purpose, as well.

Our lives and paths intertwine with those we connect with, but how we change the lives of others is sometimes a mystery. We may have a profound effect on a stranger by a simple act of kindness without ever being aware of it. On the other hand, an unthinking unkind act or act of cruelty (purposeful or inadvertent) can impact someone else's life for ill. The shifts we create in each other's lives are all part of our human experience, which in turn effects our spirituality, as well.

Some believe that our interactions with others are planned before we come here (think of the concepts of destiny and soulmates). Others believe that we come into contact with others by free will, through the many synchronicities of choices. Whichever belief you subscribe to, Lightworkers still require human connection to fulfill our spiritual mission. This is why spirits need to connect on a human level here on earth. Sometimes sensitive Lightworkers become so hurt or pained by these connections that they shut down. They think that by isolating themselves and cutting off their connections they are somehow protected or shielded from the pain that other people can bring into their lives. This is a real catch-22, though, because although isolating yourself can feel safe, it also cuts off the growth process and blocks the path you were meant to walk. This suffocates the spirit; the soul cannot grow, and light energy can no longer expand. It is through our human connections and relationships that we are able to ascend higher in our spirituality. Conversely, Lightworkers who become *too* attached to the material world also will tend operate from a place of fear. They become clingy and needy for fear of losing the physical presence of the object of their affection.

How Relationships Teach Us to Love Ourselves, or Not...

Many times our relationships will shape the view we have of ourselves. Self-esteem and self-worth can all be impacted by the relationships we form in our human incarnation. On a very basic level, children look for validation and self-worth through the love and nurturing of their parents. In early childhood, parents are what children depend on to survive and thrive. From a child's perspective, if a parent is neglectful—doesn't put time into showing the child how important he is, for example—or outright abusive, the child grows up feeling that he doesn't matter in the world.

This doesn't stop at childhood, of course. We tend to use others' feelings about and reactions to us as a mirror, a perfectly accurate reflection of *who we are*. In doing this, the highly sensitive Lightworker eventually obtains a distorted view of her authentic self. This is similar to what happens when you look into one of those carnival mirrors, where your head is huge and the rest of your body all out of proportion. This is not how we are really formed, of course, but we are forced to see ourselves through this distorted reflection. If this mirror were the only one we had to use, we would begin to believe we were really shaped that way. This illustrates how important healthy human relationships are in the way we value ourselves and keep the element of self-love and healthy self-image intact.

Some Lightworkers may actually become so attached to and comfortable with this distorted image that they refuse to see themselves any differently. So, for example, when a partner comes along who is loving and sees you for the pure and beautiful person you really are, you will continuously reveal to that person only the distorted reflection of yourself, thereby sabotaging the relationship. Of course, others will react to this, and the results will be distorted, as well.

There's just no two ways about it: Human connections affect our spiritual well-being. That said, whether others uplift and support us (helping our light energy expand), or tear us down and threaten our growth (draining our light energy and stunting our spiritual growth), we actually have control over the effects these human interactions have on our spirit and energy. Next I will show you how.

Turning the mirror around

Instead of accepting others' reactions to you as a reflection of yourself, why not choose another mirror and see yourself in the most flattering sunlight you can imagine? You are not defined by anyone else's treatment of your humanity. You are defined by your beautiful and loving spirit, and you must commit to never losing sight of this truth. Every time you feel diminished by another person in an interaction, circumstance, or relationship, why not do something to counteract that and that validates how wonderful you are? Search out the good in yourself and in humanity as a whole; that will help you connect with your authentic self, which is perfection just as it was created. Here are a few ways you can validate your inner beauty:

+ Take some time alone to appreciate your own company.

+ Help someone who is really in need.

+ Reflect on all your accomplishments and feel pride in them.

+ If you receive a compliment, accept it without any doubt of the sincerity of what was said.

+ Compliment yourself!

+ Release any blame or guilt associated with unhealthy relationships.

+ Look in the mirror and name at least three features that you love about yourself.

+ Reflect on the positive relationships in your life and give thanks for them.

+ Write a "vision statement" for yourself that does not include others (for example, that you want to be married or engaged by next year). List the achievements, goals, and dreams *you* would love to accomplish in a specific time frame.

+ Take a moment to be grateful for all the people in your life that you love and cherish. Remember that people are inherently good.

There is no need to change or mold yourself to please others—or, more to the point, to try to fix the reflection. Remember that their lenses are distorted; *you* are not. Sadly, many of my clients have difficulty letting go of this carnival mirror image. They even actively resist it. Why would someone want to hold on to this distorted reflection? My best answer is that it keeps the attachments to those who hurt them intact. They fear the process of forgiving and letting go of the person or people who caused them pain. There are many reasons for this.

Owning Human Pain From Human Connection

Some people feel that if they forgive and let go, it excuses the bad behavior or gives the victimizer a free pass. This is not true. Forgiveness is for you, not for the one who caused you pain. To forgive is to let go of the pain or the way this person perceived you and move forward with a real understanding of your authentic self, *not* the self who is damaged.

Once someone inflicts pain upon you, it becomes yours. You own it. You have now become the proud owner of spiritual, emotional, and sometimes even physical pain.

Once pain has been inflicted, you have several choices: You can hold onto the pain, maybe even nurture it and help it grow; you can let it control your life and wound you even further; or you can develop patterns to repeatedly experience the same type of pain, thus causing the pain to multiply exponentially. I will offer you another, better choice: Take ownership of this pain and take the necessary steps to eradicate it from your entire existence. Because once someone causes you pain, it becomes yours and actually has nothing to do with the person who inflicted it. Owning your own pain gives you the power to change it and heal it. There really is no use in ruminating about how or why a person hurt you. What is done cannot be undone, but you *can* heal yourself. Once you come to the point where you have taken ownership of your pain, it is now yours to do with as you please. You can choose to embrace it, experience the feeling of it, learn from it, and release it. Finally, as you come out of the darkness, you can actually feel a sense of gratitude for the connection you made with this other soul. This is a healthy way to process your pain from relationships. This will take you to a higher place, and you will be more prepared to go into another relationship unscathed.

Ownership is empowerment

Owning our pain and processing it in a healthy way is a transcendent experience! This is how we grow spiritually from human interaction, even when it is perceived as a negative experience. If we hold onto the pain, this gives us a victim mentality. We are allowing the pain to infiltrate our energy so deeply that we begin to close down. Not all human connections have to be stories with happy endings or romance novels in order for us to benefit from them spiritually, emotionally, and mentally. Although some connections can be outright painful, if we chose to experience them in a way that shifts the perspective from victimhood to a transformational process, what we once perceived as profound pain can become a source of growth and strength. Here is a five-step process for achieving growth and turning pain of the heart into expansion of your light energy:

1. **Own your pain:** Understand that once you have felt the pain of a relationship, it is now yours to deal with. You cannot release something you never take ownership of. Disregard the person who inflicted this pain. By constantly bringing him or her back into your thoughts—allowing this person to rent space in your head—you're embracing a victim mentality. This takes away your personal power. This pain is now yours, so choose how you will approach it and deal with it.

2. **Embrace your pain and actually allow yourself to feel:** Yes, you read that right. By embracing your pain, you must hold it close: Do not bury it, do not deny it, but literally embrace it even though it hurts. Feel the pain and see it through to the other side. At this phase many people feel so overwhelmed they shut down. Sometimes the feeling can even be physical. Ride it out, because in order to get to the destination you must travel the journey. If you need to cry, then cry until you have no tears left. If you need to confide in a friend, then confide. If you're process a very deep trauma, work this through carefully with a competent therapist. Just do not avoid it. If you are planning on ever getting over this, you must first actually experience it. It is very important to know this is a step in a process of growth, and you must not allow yourself to become stuck in this stage.

3. **Understand what has occurred:** Now we will come to the stage of understanding. Understanding before we are understood is important. Perhaps this person was not in the same phase of life you were in, or your desires were not in alignment. Understanding is important to the process of not taking everything personally. This experience was not all about you. Understanding the other person's perspective is important. This does not mean you should place blame on yourself, but that, perhaps, he or she had a different life plan

than the one you had attached to this relationship. Understand that it is not all about you, and what occurred was really not personally directed at you (although it sure may feel that way!).

4. **Release it:** Once we own, feel, and understand our pain, it is time to let it go. This is a step that many people find difficult. Feelings of finality come with releasing, and sometimes finality equates to forever, and that can be frightening. It doesn't necessarily mean this person is gone from your life forever (although sometimes it can and should); it simply means that you are releasing the pain associated with this person forever. Practicing forgiveness for yourself and others is important in this process. To forgive doesn't mean the person gets a free pass to inflict pain on you; it just means you are now free of the pain and you will not harbor bitterness, wish for vindication, or seek retribution. This is not your place in this stage. Your part is to forgive and allow the pain to transform into light energy.

5. **Practice gratitude:** Now that you have come to the ending step in growth through pain, you can actually emerge from the darkness and into the light. You have grown so much through this process and you have understood others and yourself. You are not holding onto bitterness, emotional baggage, or dark energy, and you are so grateful for the

experience and ready to move on to a new healthy connection.

This is all why we as spiritual beings need human connection. As we continue to connect and engage, we gain experience. We need to know ourselves and the ways in which we still need to grow. As we live through different, sometimes-painful human experiences we transform our energy over and over again, and finally come to a place in our lives of truly knowing our authentic selves. No connection is meant to drag you down or devalue you; they are all meant to build your resolve and strengthen your character so you can live out your purpose as a Lightworker. It's simple, but it isn't easy!

CHAPTER 5

How and Why We Seek Out Dysfunctional Relationships

Why is it that we always seem to find ourselves in relationships that leave us damaged or wounded? These patterns are sometimes difficult to understand, as we cycle through connection after connection that always seem to end in heartache. Do we take on the victim role and focus on the other person and his or her part? Or do we own the connections we make and take responsibility for the configurations of connections and personal alignments we make? How, practically speaking, can we own our part and understand that we do call into play the relationships in our lives? How can we ever understand the method to our relationship madness?

If we take responsibility for the way we attract the type of partners we do, we become self-aware and fully empowered to shift those connections. Owning our part means there are no victims within relationships; each player is given a choice to play his or her role. Lightworkers have a very specific method of choosing their relationships, based not only on their inherent need to be of service but also the human experiences they have endured and survived. These two imperatives can create a perilous tug of war between heaven and earth, with the Lightworker stuck in the middle.

Seeking Out Relationships That Jeopardize Our Ability to Love

The ideas of soulmates, karma, and soul contracts are all good theories. I truly believe we plan our soul group (human relationships) before we enter this lifetime. Despite our planning, however, they may not always go as we wish. The question is why and how we seek out wounded or dysfunctional relationships. Why are we so selfless to the point that we risk our own personal happiness? Is it to fulfill a calling or appease a human need/fill an inner void? As I already mentioned, our human side needs validation; it is fear-based and ego-driven, whereas the spirit side only knows love without conditions or physical attachments. With an awareness of these two distinct counterparts it's easy to understand how fear can override the loving nature of the spiritual side with the anxious attachments of the human side. So no matter what plans or contracts we may have constructed prior to our incarnation (our destiny), our preordained life *can* be altered by free will.

We all know that person who is in a relationship that makes no sense—indeed, perhaps you are that person. Perhaps you are unable to walk away from an abuser. Perhaps you are electing to stay with this person, hoping that he or she will change his or her ways. Unfortunately, this choice has likely only led to more heart chakra damage and cut off your ability to channel love energy and create healthy bonds. Why would Lightworkers, the most loving and sensitive souls on the planet, do this? Are they are only following their higher spiritual road, or are they desperately trying to validate their damaged human identity? The answer is both. The human experience can distort the best of intentions in the ways in which we seek out partners and the different methods we use to attract them.

Sometimes the spiritual self and human self can meld into a dangerous blend of fear and overwhelming urges. Fear of being unlovable (that is, of not being validated) taints this urge to follow a higher calling. We can make excuses, obfuscate, and blame others, but the simple fact is when we continuously find ourselves in negative relationship patterns, we are allowing human attachment and fear to interfere with the pure love energy. Lightworkers are naturally "dialed in" to this love energy, but the human love experience is very different. Here are some reasons that Lightworkers find themselves in repeated unhappy relationships:

We choose to be born into them. Sometimes we are born into dysfunctional families for a purpose. This begs the question of why you would choose a family that was sure to create so much unhappiness for you. We purposely choose incarnate souls with whom we have soul contracts *or* who we know will need us at some point. As a Lightworker you planned ahead of time in order to help those who would be functioning on a lower vibrational level here on earth. Lightworkers in general are just that giving and selfless and often agree to make certain sacrifices to fulfill their calling. Choosing to be born to wounded parents is something a spirit of the higher realms is inclined to make. Just by being born they can bring light energy into a very dark home. Although they may not solve any longstanding dysfunctional family issues, their healing light makes a difference that may not be visible on a superficial level. It takes a lifetime to complete their work, but when Lightworkers chose to enter into the world in order to help families already in pain, the family itself becomes the way for the Lightworker to fulfill her divine mission.

We find validation in being the one who "fixes" everything. Lightworkers are just like anyone else in that they need to feel worthwhile, that their existence has intrinsic value. No one likes to feel worthless, not even Lightworkers! So if you lack self-esteem or have a minimal sense of self-worth as a Lightworker, you may seek a partner who brings out what you feel is the best in you. This may be your ability to handle crises or other people's drama, for example. Although you may feel this makes you appear strong and capable, it is really a clear indication that you need others to validate your worth. This is untrue, of course; you need no earthly validation for your healing role, but for some reason Lightworkers like to attract partners who test the limits of their light energy.

We are seeking to relive a painful event(s) with the hope of a different outcome. Sensitive Lightworker children and young adults who have been traumatized by life events may become wounded. This sets them up to repeat the event or events and hope for a different outcome. I once had a client who became overweight in her late teens, and it continued well into her 20s. She fell in love at the age of 19 and they planned on marrying. Her "loving" finance promised her that he would set the date when she lost 50 pounds. As much as she tried, however, she was never able to keep off the weight. She would lose it and then regain it again, over and over. Her fiance became frustrated with her and eventually left her.

This set off a terribly painful cycle of her always changing herself to please a guy. If she met a new man and he loved football, suddenly she became a fan. If she met a man who was vegan, being vegan became her passion, too. After living this way for some time, she didn't even know herself anymore. Of course her efforts never really worked, yet she repeated them over and over again in hopes of winning the heart of a man. She repeated the same painful relationships over and over, hoping that one day the outcome would differ. It never did. Because the men she dated either did not love her for who she really was, or because they sensed the desperation in her and knew it was fake, they would feel hoodwinked or manipulated. The lesson? Do not try to change the past. You have nothing to prove. Release it and move forward, loving yourself more than ever.

Our empathetic nature resonates with the pain of others. Empathy is a wonderful gift, but it also means that you literally take on others' pain. Taking on pain that is not yours is a trap that many empathic souls fall into. Instead of guiding a wounded friend, partner, or family member through a healing journey, we take his or her pain as our own. (This is almost unavoidable, but there are ways to deal with this, as I will show you later in the book.)

We are unconsciously perpetuating a victim mentality. If you have ever been victimized in a relationship for any extended period of time, it's all too easy to perceive yourself as the victim in every subsequent relationship. Once you receive this image of yourself into your consciousness, it is a hard one to shake. This is yet another trap you can fall into as you see yourself through the eyes of others instead of through your own eyes, as you truly are. The trouble here is if you take on the identity of always being the victim rather than a light warrior, people *will* victimize you. If your sensitive nature has caused you to be abused over and over again, and you feel as though you've forgotten what a truly loving relationship is like, it is never too late to retrain yourself to see yourself as a victor and not a victim.

CHAPTER 6

Recognizing Our Responsibility for What We Attract

We have discussed the different ways in which Lightworkers seek out partners, not only to follow the inner imperative to heal but also to heal the wounded human experience that they themselves have survived. Now we can begin to understand our part in the situations we find ourselves in. Everything comes from a place of love and an intent to heal, so taking responsibility doesn't connote "blame"; it simply means owning our part in the relationship dynamic. In doing this we can take better control of our own actions and still be consciously aware of how we live our lives from love and pure intent. Every connection we make with another is part of our spiritual and human experience and should be cherished and considered a significant part of our personal growth.

As we reflect on each relational experience we need to ask ourselves what we take away from these relationships. Have they inspired us and/or helped us live out our own divine purpose? If the answer is no, then we have to examine the roles we assume in each experience. In this way we will begin to see the entire trajectory of our relationships in a new light. If you are contending with a difficult partnership or marriage, for example, know that you would not have drawn this person in if he or she did not fill a void or correct a wrong that you were/ are seeking to correct. Each and every connection has divine significance to you. Even if you feel that it hasn't turned out as you expected, the need was filled for its appointed time. This is not to say that fulfilling all these needs is always for your greater good, of course. As you fill a need, you may be creating more toxic energy or wounds to your spirit. Many times these voids or needs come from a place of pain and loss that you are constantly seeking to heal and address within yourself. For whatever reason, this particular partner may trigger something buried deep within you that you're already seeking to heal. Because the spirit is whole and comprised of only love, it is the human side that allows and incurs the triggers.

The Problem of Pain

From the time we are born we experience pain. Childhood traumas, hurtful words, feeling abandoned—it happens to everyone who is or ever was engaged in the human experience (in other words, everyone now living or who has ever lived on this planet). Pain is an essential part of the human experience. But it is not all for naught. Although this may sound counterintuitive or even cruel, you experience spiritual and emotional pain (I am not speaking of physical pain here) to help you grow and expand your light energy. It happens like this: We tend to seek and draw to us what we inherently need. It happens like water flowing into a lower place: Gravity pulls it in, and it naturally flows into the place that it must fill. The same principle applies to the people you draw into your life: They are the water (the energy) that fills the ditches (the needs) of your body, mind, and soul. When you cannot find a way to stop toxic energy from encroaching, it creates an overflow that spills over into all other aspects of your life. So, yes, we attract the energy—both good and bad—that we need to fill our voids, but we must also take the responsibility of stopping it when it becomes a painful overflow that ends up choking life rather than giving it.

Processing pain

How we process the pain experience will determine how much we progress and grow spiritually. If we do not process pain properly, our own energy will become stuck, and the water that fills our ditches will just sit there and become stagnant. Stagnation causes our energy to become toxic, and we will constantly seek to clear it or heal it, somehow get it flowing again. This involves processing pain, and it is much easier said than done.

If we look back on our entire human experience, often we can identify our empty places and connect the dots to find what causes us to "call in," or manifest, certain types of relationships. Our spirits are strategically designed to manifest whatever we truly lack in our spirit, not what we *think* we want. For example, we may be praying or asking (begging?) for the perfect mate, yet constantly meet with the same types of dysfunctional people. This happens because sometimes the human ego (which, again, constantly needs validation) can distort the message; we simply cannot "dial in" to our own voids properly. The message goes out into the universe, and the universe delivers your order, bringing you the very same person, event, or situation that created the void in the first place—all because you are seeking to re-create and correct, because you never truly healed in the first place.

Naturally, this creates unhealthy patterns in relationships. For example, if we suffer from low self-esteem, our human ego will search to re-create similar relationship challenges that created the initial pain experience in a bid to strive for a different outcome. Unfortunately this usually only results in basically the same outcome that helped you develop the pain in the first place, and in fact only serves to deepen it.

Healing others

Many Lightworkers have relationship issues because they get sucked into this repetitive cycle. They are like a hamster in a wheel, constantly moving but getting nowhere fast when it comes to processing their pain and healing their relationships. Our inner need to heal others and be of service is a constant, quiet calling within us; the urge is always there to heal those who are wounded. The problem is, those who are wounded, energy vampires, and those who could best be described as narcissists sense your abundant light energy and are naturally drawn to it. A Lightworker without a strong sense of who he is and his own power is easy prey for these types. This is why it is so important to recognize your power as a light being. You are not a victim; you are a powerful healer, and this is why you have come here to the planet at this time. Letting your guard down and allowing ill-intentioned people to drain your light energy will prevent you from fulfilling your life purpose. Moreover it will bring on feelings of unworthiness that will keep you from accepting the love you deserve.

Own your pain

Once we recognize our voids and the pain we are harboring, it's time to own the pain. In my work many clients come to me reluctant to own their wounds. They seem to embrace and even revel in the victim role, and keep rehashing how they were hurt or unfairly treated, refusing to move on from the point in time when the pain occurred. The first step to healing is understanding that you now own this festering wound and it is yours and yours alone to heal. Although you can point a finger at the person who originally hurt you, the pain and spiritual injury is now yours. I liken it to the common cold. Although a coughing coworker "gave" you her cold, the cold is now yours to cure! You'll need to rest, take some aspirin, eat chicken soup, maybe even see a doctor, whatever will help you to get better. Your coworker, although she is "to blame" in the sense that she passed the cold to you, cannot help you heal physically. Similarly, an ex-lover who broke your heart cannot help you heal spiritually or emotionally. Letting go of what happened on a physical level and understanding that you have a spiritual wound that is yours to heal is the first step. Sometimes, owning your pain is as simple as filling your own voids and casting aside the idea that someone else is going to fill them for you. This is really taking responsibility for the healing process before you engage with someone else.

Releasing techniques are a big part of the healing process, too. This involves releasing the guilt you are carrying from what happened. "Maybe I could have done something differently" or "Maybe I'm just not worthy of a happy relationship because I made mistakes in my past"—this type of thinking is counterproductive and will not help you own or release the pain. All your experiences brought you to where you are today for a reason. There is no fault or blame in love, only ways to build your fortitude and expand your light energy, even if the relationship was wholly unsuccessful. Whatever happened to you was "meant" to happen in the sense that it was designed to bring you to a place where you could find your ultimate partner. The choice is yours: You can linger in guilt or victimization, or you can find the value in the relationship and move forward with only love in your heart, knowing that your perfect partner is ultimately the final destination on this journey.

Allowing yourself to feel your pain is a big, admittedly unpleasant part of the journey. Just as we speak of energetic polarities (light and dark, high frequency and low frequency, etc.) as a necessary force in the universe, pain is necessary to experience joy! Of course no one *wants* to feel pain (unless the person is a masochist), but in order to achieve a healthy balance, you need to experience both ends of the spectrum. Know that your heart chakra will expand and light energy will enter it in leaps and bounds, when you successfully own, feel, and heal your wounds. This journey is unavoidable, so the sooner we understand we need to travel through the dark places to get to the light, the faster we'll get there! It is not an easy journey by any means, and many Lightworkers tend to avoid it, but there are no shortcuts to healing, so we must travel through our darkness to get to the healing place.

✦

PART III

✦

PART III

CHAPTER 7

Where There Is Love, Pain Cannot Exist

A s we have discussed, Lightworkers need to balance their inner spiritual calling with their human side to achieve equity in their relationships. We have differentiated the love energy (spiritual type) from the love experience (human type). Clearly it is not the love energy that hurts; it is the ego-driven human experience that creates pain. Thus, no pain can exist within the authentic love-energy source that Lightworkers channel. So we will need to look at how both our human side and our spiritual side understand the true source of love energy.

If we examine the human love experience, we can see it is fear-driven. The human ego is fueled by fear, and your human identity is always vulnerable to this fear because it's always aware of its transient existence. So the human identity will be manipulated easily by the ego. The ego always fears risking its security and wants to take charge of the relationship because it is also very controlling. Authentic love energy, on the other hand, wants to step in and put an end to the egotistical, fear-driven love experience. This is because spirit is fearless.

So there really is an internal battle going on between spirit and humanity whenever we engage in relationships. The human identity will win if the Lightworker is not in touch with her higher self, or spirit. Most often a fear-driven relationship will not survive. When a relationship is purely ego-driven, insecurity, jealousy, possessiveness, and control issues begin to take a stronghold. This creates pain and is not the true essence of love. As you may have surmised, there has to be a balance of both spiritual and human love to make it work. That means learning to give and receive love equally and, most importantly, loving as fearlessly as you can.

Mortality and the Transient Image of the Self

For the human side, love equates to a physical connection. By this I do not mean merely a sexual connection, but love that is felt for the actual physical incarnation of another soul. When the physical is involved, loss is automatically a possibility. The physical state of being is only a temporary situation; we eventually lose everything that is of the physical world. It is just the natural process of existing on the physical plane. Things get old, they wear out, they die; it is ultimately going to happen to each and every aspect of your physical world: your possessions, your friends, your pets, your own body. By contrast, spiritual love is eternal, authentic love that comes from oneness with our source creator. It can never be lost because it is divine energy, and energy never dies. Once you understand that we are all one, part of the same divine source, it is easy to see how you can never lose a loved one, because we are essentially a part of this unconditional love source, which comes from creator. What is eternal can never be lost; therefore spiritual love knows no fear of loss and no pain, nor does it require any action to sustain it. It simply is...for all eternity.

Sensitive Lightworkers need to begin to view their time here on earth as more of a temporary situation, a place where we have come to be of service, grow spiritually, and prepare for a glorious place in eternity. This physical plane is not home. We all know this intuitively, but our human side still fears losing it all, including the love experience. All forms of physical love incite an inner fear of loss within us. Even though our spirit understands that this is a temporary situation, the experience of love for our spirit's human counterpart brings on a bit of a panic and with it the feeling of needing to do something to hold onto it. Remember that for the spirit, love and energy will merge together to guide us along our path to ascension or create a perfect storm for energy wounds.

Overcoming the Fear of Loss

The only pure form of love is the spiritual type. The human type of love is more of an "experience" than it is the authentic form of love that comes from universal energy, the most powerful force in the universe. But when we engage in a romantic love experience, for example, it creates intense energy that can shake us at the very foundation of our humanness. Just imagine an experience that "calls in" the triggers of old energetic wounds, stimulates our physical senses and sexuality, and then brings in the mighty ego to add more than a touch of fear. There's a perfect storm for you! The human side of love is not something that mere mortals have an easy time navigating. This is a powerful confluence of the emotional, the spiritual, and the physical, and you will need an intense awareness of your authentic self to create an effective opportunity for spiritual growth and personal happiness. The experience of human love creates energy (just as everything we do, say, or think does), but no matter what the outcome of the relationship, we should always strive for an outcome that ultimately expands our light energy.

As already mentioned, life is loss. Fears from the ego are formed from the time we are born and are incurred continuously throughout life. As we grow and begin to form our own identity, we experience loss on even more complex levels. For example, we may lose our place in the family unit when a sibling is born; and we lose our place as a free-spirited explorer of life when we go to school and learn to conform to society. Human loss is an ongoing process, and we must face and accept it in order to grow. We learn that loss equates to pain, but without loss we could never make room for new growth. You can begin to view loss as not so much a setback, but a setup for you to move into the next phase of your life.

It's not easy to see loss or pain in this way. We are raised and conditioned to fear and avoid all loss. Loss of our finances, loss of our material possessions, loss of our health, loss of a loved one. These are all material fears. As we grapple with them, we often neglect to identify the things that are eternal and that we can never lose. Shifting our perspective and focusing on what can never be taken from us— real love, our faith, our spirit—will help assuage your fears of losing it all because of a relationship. If we continue to see pain as merely a painful experience and nothing more, it becomes very difficult to move forward. Seeing pain as a blessing and an opportunity to get on the path for your greater good is a *major* shift in your perception and a total game-changer in relationships. This is because it removes the element of fear and puts in its place a plan for growth.

So pain is good?

The human experience of love, particularly romance, often brings disappointment and emotional pain. When we lose a person we feel intense love for, the heartache is emotionally and even physically devastating. Again this is your human ego triggering the fears of loss that you have amassed since you came to the planet. Some very sensitive people refuse to move forward from loss and become so traumatized that they begin to associate their own identity *with* loss and abandonment, thus setting off cycles of constantly searching to fix the abandonment or loss issues by engaging in dysfunctional relationships. They are essentially replaying the same painful experiences over and over again with different partners. If you look closely at their lives and choices you will begin to see the similarities and patterns.

You may ask yourself why you keep repeating your pain. It is likely because you are out of touch with your authentic self. Until you become aware of your true self, you will constantly be setting yourself up with partners who are wounded themselves. You do this in an effort to "fix" each new partner, "make" him or her stay, and recoup the prior loss or losses. This sets the stage for a major Lightworker meltdown. However, as I mentioned in the previous chapter, if you process your pain in a healthy way, the pain can be transformational into something positive and beneficial to all. Pain then becomes a direct path to self-discovery.

So in this sense pain is indeed a very good thing. As long as we own it and process it into something positive, it can be an illuminating experience that will shine light instead of diminishing it. There's really no avoiding it, so you may as well learn from it! Lightworkers need to practice the human love experience because it helps them to expand their light energy and is essential for their growth. Pain, when handled properly, equates to growth. Remember: It is only when you hold on to the painful sense of loss that is naturally associated with this human love experience that you begin to shut down or develop unhealthy behavior patterns while trying to heal the loss experience. Who wants to hold onto pain? What a relief it would be to just let it go. You should honor yourself enough to allow that to happen.

Transforming the Energy

Hopefully by now you understand that the human love experience will always end in loss, either through a temporary separation, insurmountable obstacles, or, ultimately, physical death. This all sounds very frightening and kind of hopeless, doesn't it? But it doesn't have to be. Let's strive to understand personal relationships and bonds with others on a new level. You may feel a resistance to this "new" concept of love and life, but deep within your Lightworker spirit, you already know it to be true. I am just assisting you in remembering. Being a Lightworker is about knowing who you are and why you are here in this particular place and time. As you get to know your authentic self as more than just your human self, you are more than just "Jane" or "Richard" or someone's secretary or someone's father. You are a spiritual being, part of an almighty source creator and a collective army of light warriors who are here with a mission to complete. *You have a divine purpose.* You are one with all there is and you hold the power of the collective. It is possible to transform energy and transmute your fears into a belief—a *knowing*—that within that powerful place of connectivity and oneness, pain and loss do not exist. Once you understand your authentic self, both you and your powers will be limitless. Living each experience as an opportunity or vehicle for growth, rather than just a random series of events that happen "to" you, will only empower you. You will be able to master your Lightworker role with ease.

This shift or transformation must be incorporated into your conscious thought process constantly. The shift won't occur if you keep allowing yourself to slip back into the wounded human identity. Keeping your inner dialogue loving and supportive and opening up to communication with the higher planes of intelligence will help prevent you from falling back into the outdated thought patterns of the fear-driven human you thought you were. Your new perspective will allow you to see a much bigger picture, seeing yourself as so much more than the flesh and blood that you've been identifying with, the human side. Your true essence is eternal and goes way beyond the physical shell you are housed in right now. Your new perspective will be a gift; you will feel supported in your journey knowing that all situations come to you for the purpose of your greater good. You will look at relationships with a more loving and insightful awareness. You will not feel the pain of loss or abandonment anymore, and you will understand that all those who come into your life, no matter what length of time they stay, have come to enhance your journey, not harm or wound you.

This shift in perspective will expand your light energy and will have a transformational effect on the energy you create from the human love experience. You will see a definite change for the better in all your relationships when you make this shift. You will shine brighter from within, your vitality for life will be apparent for all to see, and personal relationships will be more fulfilling. This is because as you expand your light energy, you automatically open the gates that will allow goodness to flow into your life. When you put out light energy, like a magnet you attract more light energy, and a glorious cycle will take effect, much like what many call the "Law of Attraction." You will attract partners who are in alignment with your energetic vibration. Keeping your vibration high will attract like-minded people who will enhance your life in all areas, including what most people desire: romantic love and acceptance. Familial and work relationships will also feel the effect of this energetic shift. More opportunities will come your way, and wounds from childhood will begin to heal.

Things to remember

Here are some things to keep in mind when you are seeking to create transformational shifts when it comes to your energy and engaging with others.

There is no pain in the love energy; it is the human ego that manifests the pain.

When disappointed in someone always look for the silver lining. There is a hidden blessing in everything.

Do not attach outcomes or expectations to relationships (i.e., commitment, marriage, or even failure); simply allow relationships to develop organically.

Do not allow possessiveness over another person to set in. Each person is the master of his or her life.

See human interactions on a deeper level; question how the other person helps you grow spiritually, even if your human side perceives the relationship as negative.

Remember the concept of oneness: We are all part of the collective, and there is no separation within divine oneness.

Nothing is ever lost in the universe; separations from loved ones are only temporary.

Relationships have a life span; whether long or short in duration, all bonds will accomplish the divine purpose they were meant to accomplish.

Accept what is without resistance. Relationship energy is like the tides: As the energy flows, you need to flow with it.

Remember the other person has a divine mission, as well, and you must not enforce your will to interfere with this.

Do not take the words or actions personally. Others have triggers and festering wounds, too. If someone hurts you, pray for the other person's healing.

Chapter 8

On the Road to Good Intentions

As Lightworkers we come to the planet to heal through the power of love. There is always an inner calling to be of service and to spread our light energy to those around us. Here are just a few of the typical traits and experiences of Lightworkers:

+ A strong inner urge to help or heal others.

+ Situations that may not involve them directly, affect them on a deep emotional level.

✦ Feelings of empathy for others.

✦ The feeling of wanting to help solve global issues.

✦ Feeling a need to "fix" problems for others, even when such problems don't involve them.

✦ Feeling a need to nurture or care for all living creatures (animals, plants, etc.).

✦ Being extra sensitive to external stimuli.

✦ Feeling alone and isolated much of the time.

• Experiencing premonitions or prophetic visions or dreams.

These are just some of the many traits of sensitive Lightworkers. As a Lightworker you have a selfless inner calling to be of service. When we speak of these traits in terms of personal relationships, it is important to harness these inner urges and set healthy boundaries in order to have a happy life, not only as a Lightworker but as a regular person. As we already discussed, the human identity and the spiritual identity need to work together in harmony in order for the Lightworker to master his or her role. If the human identity is continuously wounded by the spiritual Lightworker's actions, toxic energy will begin to accumulate in the physical body and bring on unpleasant side effects, which commonly manifest in physical illness. It is a fact that a Lightworker who has come to work on the earth plane must carry out her mission in a physical body. To do this, spirit and humanity must work in harmony. Indeed, one cannot work without the other. As well, both counterparts need to receive love equally, as love begets love energy.

Managing Empathy

One of the Lightworker's most powerful gifts is empathy. Lightworkers can immediately understand how others are feeling. If someone is in pain, the Lightworker literally feels this person's pain and instinctively responds to it. Either the Lightworker tries to fix the pain or he tries to shoulder the burden for the other person. This wonderful quality that you have is a gift, but it also has a dark side. The pain you take on from others will create energy in your own life that is reflective of others' pain. Lightworkers sometimes mistake this pain energy as a feeling that belongs to them. Learning to manage empathy in relationships is key in maintaining a healthy energy field for the Lightworker.

If you are constantly taking in your partner's wounded energy as your own, you will eventually go into toxic overload and spiral into a very dark place. So, yes, empathy is an amazing gift and a wonderful quality, but when not controlled it opens you up to being overburdened, overwhelmed, and easily manipulated by others who know you will carry their load for them. Empathy misused is no longer a gift but a burden that is not authentically our own. If not managed properly, empathy can actually change the course of your life from that of a light warrior to someone who is a victim of his own good intentions.

In this chapter we will discuss ways to be empathic and still maintain your own sense of self, not taking on the problems or responsibilities of others.

Lightworkers are kind, gentle, and loving by nature. But they are also powerful warriors of the light, and that does not always include being polite. If you feel you're being unkind by not absorbing the pain of others, you're incorrect. By taking on their pain you're denying them the chance to heal their wounds and process their own toxic energy. You may have the best of intentions in empathizing and feeling their pain, but you cannot allow this empathy to take away your personal happiness and light energy in the process. The good news is that how you use this empathy gift is entirely under your control. You can use it to represent the light or allow it to drag you down with the emotional and spiritual baggage of others. Learning to recognize when you are empathizing to the point of literally embodying the pain of others will come as you find your authenticity and personal boundaries. As you travel this road to self-discovery and healing, you will see when you are overextending this gift, know when to use it, and know when empathy is interfering not only with your divine mission but your human experience, as well. Managing all your sensitivities will begin to be a part of your daily practice and journey to self-love, and you will see the fruits of this reflected in all your relationships.

Empathy run amok: choosing wounded partners

When a Lightworker enters into a relationship she will usually take on the role of healer. A lot can go wrong when choosing a relationship partner who is wounded. Often the boundaries are not put in place to ensure an equal, balanced connection, and the Lightworker becomes rapidly depleted, with her human identity now becoming the wounded one. This creates the toxic energy we discussed that manifests as undesirable physical symptoms.

Despite the risks, Lightworkers are often drawn to the walking wounded. Addicts, control freaks, narcissists, egomaniacs, deviants, miscreants, sociopaths, and other undesirable or dangerous types may look like Prince Charming or Miss Fairytale Princess to the Lightworker. It is in the Lightworker's nature to find a target and "inflict" all her gifts upon this person. (I use the word *inflict* because, most often, you will do more harm than good to both you and your partner.) Mixing the human love experience with the healing love energy can result in enabling the wounded partner to stay in a place of pain and not heal his or her energetic wounds. The Lightworker is no longer objective in her role as a healer because she has allowed her human ego to step in and take over.

Another thing to consider is that a Lightworker who is experiencing human ego-driven love can become selfish in the way he imposes healing on a partner who just isn't ready to heal. The dysfunction works both ways! People who are wounded or harboring toxic energy need to come to the point of *wanting* to heal, wanting to dig in deep and heal the festering wounds of their past. This is not a pleasant or easy undertaking, and the Lightworker's partner may be resistant to the healing process, setting off a battle of the wills that is played out over and over again in the arena of their relationship.

My client Cynthia was deeply in love with a man named Stanley. Cynthia was a highly self-aware Lightworker, and even though she was my client she had her own spiritual practice giving intuitive advice to others; she was wonderful at her job! Stanley suffered from an addiction to prescription medication and alcohol. She was not aware of this when they met and fell in love. Although we later discovered in her sessions that her spirit had known he was wounded from the start, her human ego refused to see it because she was so madly in love with Stanley—or so she thought. Stanley had been abandoned by his mother (who also suffered addictions) when he was 3 years old and carried the contaminating wounds of his childhood into his adult life. The emotional and spiritual pain caused him to self-medicate with booze and pills, and become addicted. The union was a dangerous situation for both Stanley and Cynthia to be in. She was constantly trying to heal him with unconditional love, then tough love, then energetic healing love, and on and on with no success. They would break up and make up frequently, and the relationship became the equivalent of an emotional roller coaster. How could a Lightworker who was so successful in her work with her clients be such a failure at healing the one she loved most?

The simple truth was Cynthia was not a failure at all. It was just that Stanley was not at the point of wanting to heal. As the saying goes, you can lead a horse to water but you can't make him drink. Stanley refused to drink of Cynthia's healing energy. She became frustrated and began to feel unworthy of love, as often happens when a Lightworker doesn't succeed in her mission. Eventually she herself became wounded, and the dysfunctional cycle developed. When Cynthia asked me why she couldn't seem to maintain a healthy romantic relationship, I explained to her that she put herself in an inappropriate role with Stanley. She was not his healer, and she couldn't be objective in her role as his girlfriend or his healer anymore, because her own human ego and the human love experience had been brought into play. By remaining in the relationship she was actually enabling Stanley to stay in his wounded place while creating wounds in her own energy. Having exhausted her light energy Cynthia finally had to take a stand, take a step back, and look at the relationship from an objective point of view. In the end she decided to part ways with Stanley for good. Once she did this, she was able to begin the healing process for herself. Through our sessions she finally understood that despite her best intentions, she could not heal someone who was invested in holding onto pain and remaining in a dark place. Stanley just wasn't ready to unearth all the pain from his childhood and process through it.

Some people never get to the place of excavating their wounds. Understandable, as it's a frightening and painful process. It's like journeying through a dark tunnel never knowing when you will see the light at the end. Lightworkers like Cynthia will do their best to live up to the challenge and will stay in these kinds of situations for years, trying over and over again unsuccessfully to heal their wounded loved ones. As well intentioned as they are, a Lightworker can be just as stubborn when it comes to her divine mission! At times an unhealthy obsession with the wounded partner can begin to take hold of the Lightworker, and then she becomes stuck in a place of darkness from which it is difficult to escape. So what is the solution? Read on.

We All Have Wounds

It goes without saying that it is very unlikely if not impossible to find a partner who has absolutely no wounds from the past. It is perfectly okay to have wounds; indeed, as we already discussed, healing our wounds is how we grow and expand our light energy. But putting yourself in the role of healer with your partner is overstepping the boundaries of the human love experience, and the relationship will never be a healthy, balanced union. Ask yourself if you are often in these types of scenarios in your personal relationships; this goes for all types of relationships, not just romantic. As you do so, consider the following statements when it comes to your relationships with family, friends, and coworkers:

- ✦ I often feel I am doing all the "work" in this relationship.
- ✦ I often feel my partner/family member/ friend doesn't understand my needs.
- ✦ I often feel undervalued by this person.
- ✦ I often feel that my loving gestures are unappreciated.
- ✦ I often feel insecure or jealous when my partner shows someone else attention.
- ✦ In many ways I feel I let this person down.
- ✦ I feel like I give too much in this relationship, with little to show for it in return.
- ✦ I always find myself always attracting or being attracted to the "undesirables."
- ✦ In my relationships I always feel like there is something missing.

Although you likely feel an urge or inner calling to help those in need, this urge is not always totally compatible with your own human needs. Sometimes a Lightworker will overlook his own needs in order to assist others on their journey, but this is counterproductive to the Lightworker's divine purpose. Of course, being a Lightworker does not mean you don't have needs of your own. One essential need is to receive an equal amount of love energy as what you put out. When we continuously place ourselves in the role of healer in personal relationships, we become depleted, and it is difficult if not impossible for us to be productive in our light work.

All Things in Moderation

In my work with Lightworkers I find that once they have a conscious awareness of what they are taking part in, they can begin to take the necessary steps to correct boundary issues or misguided intentions. A big part of this involves remembering that their human side has needs and that they must receive love as much as they give it. Always choosing a wounded partner is, in a way, a spiritual choice. If you find you do this frequently or you are not attracted to partners who are healthy in most aspects, you are allowing your spiritual mission to overtake your entire human existence. This does not bring you balance, and a Lightworker out of balance cannot function in her Lightworker capacity.

It is very unlikely that a highly polarized relationship without boundaries will bring you happiness. A clear awareness of your own needs as a human with human emotions is something that requires balancing your spiritual awareness with your human ego. All things in moderation. As a Lightworker living here on the earth, you cannot live in a polarized state of "one side or another." You must find the middle ground and balance your spiritual and human needs equitably. This is not something that you do and get it over with; it is a constant process of adjusting, maintaining self-awareness, and always taking the "temperature" of your relationships. It's hard work, but worth it!

CHAPTER 9

The Cycle of Disconnect

We have discussed how Lightworkers attract wounded partners and the reasons why this happens. But what happens when Lightworkers become depleted of their light energy, and their heart chakra closes up and shuts down their ability to channel love energy?

As Lightworkers, unknowingly or knowingly we tend to put ourselves in situations with others that set us up to be the caretaker, the healer, the nurturer. Even when our partners do not want to be healed, we will literally exhaust ourselves persisting in trying to heal their inner wounds. Ultimately with a partner who refuses to process their toxic energy, we fail in our mission. This creates a feeling of being unworthy of our sacred purpose. So we begin to shut down. This can happen over the course of many months or years of constantly placing ourselves in the role of healer when we should be in the role of the beloved, friend, or colleague. Keep in mind that this can also happen because of a traumatic event as well. We find it hard to make the shift from giver to acceptor of love. So the cycle of shutting down begins, and we begin to close ourselves off to new relationships, new interactions, and new bonds with others as a defense mechanism.

Because Lightworkers come to earth with the divine mission to channel light energy through the heart chakra, their natural inclination is to protect this channel at all costs, even if it means shutting it down completely. As this chakra closes up, toxic energy is trapped within it, which creates a festering wound. Even so, Lightworkers will do anything to protect their most sacred conduit, the heart chakra, even if it means placing it under lock and key along with the toxic energy they gathered from the human love experience. Once you've closed off your channel to love energy, you begin to feel the effects, such as feeling devalued as a spiritual being and human being due to the misuse of your gifts. Once Lightworkers closes themselves off and put up those walls, no one can get through. They become unhappy, closed off, and just miserable to be around.

There are physical effects, as well. The Lightworker may begin to have physical pains, and may even gain weight (usually as a protective device). They will engage in behaviors such as unhealthy eating, and embrace a sedentary lifestyle or other negative habits that affect their living environment, such as hoarding or not taking pride in their space. In effect, when a Lightworker shuts down her ability to accept the love energy of the universe, the human experience begins to suffer greatly.

As their heart chakra begins to close up, Lightworkers no longer have the ability to heal or connect with others in any kind of healthy way. What begins to happen is they put up an emotional wall that no one can penetrate. They often find themselves feeling lost, disconnected from the world, or depressed, even suicidal. So how can you keep your love energy balanced in such a way that both your spirit and your humanity thrive?

Variations of the love energy

We already know that a Lightworker's soul and purpose are driven by the love energy of the universe. When we speak of love energy, it is not just a singular, energetic force; it is multi-vibrational and comes in many forms. It is important to incorporate more than one form of this vibration into your energy or you will become unhealthily hyper-focused on just one aspect, and your energy, unbalanced. Here are the six main vibrational forms of love energy that you can channel to help keep your energy in a healthy balance. All six are necessary in creating a balanced life, and each brings a lovely individual vibration all its own. Like a guitar, each "string" or form strikes its own singular note, yet you need all six "strings" (types) to create chords and music. Here are the six main types of love energy with their Greek names along with their descriptions:

1. Philio: feeling of close friendship or familial connection.

2. Eros: named after the Greek god of fertility; romantic and lust filled.

3. Ludus: playful love, puppy love, or comaraderie.

4. Pragma: mature love, usually develops between couples married many years.

5. Philautia: self-love.

6. Agape: universal love of the creator, oneness.

Human beings need to engage in all six types of love in order to have a balanced energy flow in the heart chakra. When this gets thrown off, cycles of disconnection can emerge. For example, when I was going through a difficult divorce I fought hard to keep my spirit from closing down, but it did—for a while. I focused on my children as I put myself into survival mode. Love and romance definitely were not something I desired at that time, even though I was a young woman who naturally should have desired companionship. My sensitive nature was so traumatized by the divorce I shut down for five full years. During the fifth year, the only love I would accept was the "Philio" type from and for my children.

I became hyper-focused on my children, which in turn created anxiety because I had lost my balance. If you become overly focused on just one type of love energy, it can transform and begin to channel through another chakra. The love energy becomes distorted because it is now coming from a place of fear. As I became hyper-focused on the Philio type of love (overly invested in family and children), I actually began to channel this energy through my root chakra. This displaced love energy was still coming through, but not from the proper sources. Like trying to push a square peg into a round hole, this love did not "fit" the root chakra channel properly. Interestingly during that time I experienced a lot of lower back issues such as sciatica and muscle spasms.

In retrospect I can see how I shut out the different forms of love energy, and how being so out of balance affected me physically, emotionally, and in other ways. My anxiety and hyper-focus on my children affected them as well. As much I attempted to mask my anxiety, it rubbed off on them, and they became clingy and protective of me for a while. In adult relationships you can actually push the subject of this hyper-focusing away from you. The frustrations that come with these types of situations cloud your intuition and your spiritual gifts. Perhaps you become so hyper-focused on one person that you become blinded to the signs and messages from your guides or higher self and lose your way. It is never a good thing to focus solely on one person, project, or area of your life. Sensitive Lightworkers need to continually monitor, transform, and balance their energy flow to keep it healthy. Becoming hyper-focused doesn't allow for energetic transformation, and we become more and more unbalanced. This creates more trauma, and the cycle of disconnection continues until we either totally isolate ourselves or continually end up in unhealthy relationships.

Lack of faith

As we become disconnected, we lose our sense of support and protection from our source creator. This is because when you disconnect from love, you are also closing off to your faith in the divine. When the disconnect reaches this level, Lightworkers can feel as if they are freefalling through life, and they tend to view anything that occurs as random and proof of their victimization. The image of yourself as a victim takes away your power to heal your life or those of others. Feeling victimized puts you in a helpless position, and your natural spiritual gifts become disabled.

If this is happening to you, remember that you were put here to do sacred work, and this role you have chosen is never without divine support or protection. Our source creator would not put you here to be victimized by random attacks or pain. Everything you experience in your human form has a divine purpose. Each situation brings you opportunity to heal others and expand your light energy.

It just depends on how you view it. If you refuse to see your life as purpose driven, you will feel perpetually victimized and without support. But when you see yourself as a being who is holy and here to fulfill a sacred role, you will begin to feel empowered and protected. As you can see, keeping your faith system strong is so important. When we allow the support of and connection to the divine to penetrate our lives, we can feel unstoppable. All things are possible when we allow the divine to work magic in our lives. The key word is *allow*; we need to invite and allow this magic into our lives to experience the joy it brings.

As humans we often are reminded of our mortality and thus become attached to time frames. Keep in mind that the time frames we often put on outcomes are usually fear-driven and thus are not for our greatest good. An example would be *I need to be married by the age of 30* or *I have to reconnect with my father before it's too late*. These types of ideas are fear-driven because we fear we will run out of time. Time itself is an illusion. When we keep the mindset that we are eternal, just as our creator is, there is no need for time frames. All things will occur in the perfect timing. Moreover, when we feel the need to control events by setting time frames driven by fear, we oftentimes are setting ourselves up for disappointment. Having the faith that divine timing is at play in all your relationships will help you release your fears and that image of being a victim. The less we attempt to control, the more likely it is that things will happen in their own, perfect timing, at the most appropriate juncture in your life. If we force events or try to leverage a response from the universe, we usually regret it later because we made choices based on fear instead of going with the flow and allowing divine timing to take its proper place.

Another way to ensure that you're not propagating cycles of disconnect is to practice total acceptance of what occurs as for your greatest good. In my case I had to end a 10-year relationship because it was ultimately going to destroy my spirit. The divorce left me feeling like a failure, bitter and closed off. If I only could have understood that ending the marriage did not equate to failure and that choosing to leave was actually a really brave thing to do. People who make brave decisions aren't failures; they are actually heroes in their own lives. By leaving that situation, I made the brave choice to expand and grow spiritually and in my human identity. Ultimately I was a victor, not a victim of what outwardly appeared to be a very unfortunate situation. The ultimate truth is although it was a difficult road, it brought me to the place I am today. It strengthened my character, heightened my resolve, and put me on the path to my life's purpose. Although it took five years, I found my way out of the darkness. I was searching for the light; I always believed that things would get better and that I made my choices for a reason. This belief, along with my love for my daughters, is what held me up through the dark places. I knew my daughters depended on me, and deep in my soul I knew I had to hold out hope or I would be destroyed. If that happened, where would that leave my children? I knew this yet I still continued to live in darkness.

It took a very dramatic turn to get me out of that place of darkness and disconnect. This manifested physically in a form that was far more life threatening than the back pain I already mentioned. In 2001, five years after my divorce, and after all the stress I had endured for more than 15 years in this toxic relationship, I began to experience painful skin eruptions on my legs. These infections or boils were painful and reoccurred for about a month. Busy with my life, I didn't think much of it until suddenly, one day, I fell severely ill with a fever of 104 degrees and severe vomiting. I could barely move. My mother came to check me and said, "Well, you must have the flu." Days passed and I wasn't getting better. My fever remained elevated and I began to experience what looked like hemorrhagic petechiae—little broken blood vessels that spread in a rash all over my body. My body ached so badly that I couldn't be touched. As I lay there, I thought, *I am dying. I am afraid.* Just recalling this experience makes me shake. After five days the skin on my fingers began to peel off and I didn't have the strength to get up to use the bathroom. Finally my mother said, "Enough is enough—you're going to the hospital!"

That day was a haze, but I knew the doctors were puzzled as they examined me, with this strange rash, high fever, and my blood pressure now tanking at 50/90. After two days and several specialists, I was diagnosed with toxic shock syndrome. They had no idea how or why I had become toxic, but they began intensive intravenous antibiotics and kept me for two weeks until I was able to beat the infection. Can your body become toxic from harboring toxic energy? I think I am proof of this! But here comes the silver lining. After my recovery my entire life changed; I figuratively woke up. I understood that life is a gift and that I had to let go of the past and pain that I had endured. My body hadn't let me down. When I got sick I think my physical body was just filled to capacity with toxic energy; it simply had to be released, albeit in a physically violent way. Obviously my spirit was resistant to releasing it, so my body was stepping in and attempting to channel it all out by itself. As my body slowly healed, my spirit did, too. Not long after this I was able to allow a loving man into my life who eventually became my husband.

Now, don't get the idea you have to experience a life-threatening illness to release toxic energy from relationships! I firmly believe this would not have happened if I had processed the pain out instead of holding onto it. If I had only known how to release it or was even aware that I was holding on to it in the first place, I believe I would not have gotten so ill. You and only you can release the pain from relationships, past or present, that you are carrying.

In the next chapter I will discuss what happens when we shut down or refuse to release toxic energy, as well as which techniques you should practice to release the pain that comes from being in a constant cycle of disconnection. I'll also show you how to channel the love energy on all six vibrational levels we discussed, to help keep a healthy balance in your life.

CHAPTER 10

Isolation and Closing Doors

When the heart chakra finally closes the Lightworker will disconnect from healthy relationships almost completely. As we discussed this sets off a very harmful cycle that eventually leads to a total breakdown. In my case I suffered severe anxiety, an unhealthy hyper-focus on my children, back pain, and, eventually, a life-threatening illness. This did not happen overnight. I was unaware of the warning signs that I had closed off my channel to the love-energy of the universe. It's not only about the disconnection from other people; it's also about the importance of keeping your energy balanced and incorporating all the different levels of vibrational love into your life to be well-rounded and maintain balance.

We already know that Lightworkers are super sensitive, have difficulty resisting those in need, and sometimes refuse to accept light energy for themselves, but how do we know when we have shut down? How can we recognize that we have disconnected from others and cut off a healthy flow of love energy? As was the case for me, shutting down can sometimes go unrecognized until a total energy meltdown occurs due to excessive buildup of toxic energy. Of course, this shutting down kept me closed off from the beneficial light energy as well. Shutting down is equivalent to boarding up the windows in your house and sealing all the doors shut. No sunlight can enter, no fresh air. The air becomes stagnant and musty. The environment becomes unhealthy as everything locked inside deteriorates and rots. Eventually the house will suffer disrepair and become a toxic place to live. That boarded-up house, once so welcoming and livable, is just like the inside of a closed-up heart chakra.

In this chapter I'll discuss some patterns you may see when you are closed down to healthy love energy.

Hoarding and Hiding

Many of my clients come to me seeking clarity on relationship issues. Some find it nearly impossible to find one; others are in an unhealthy relationship. They do not realize that they are sensitive Lightworkers who have shut themselves down. They disguise the fact that they are avoiding bonding or human connection through behaviors or life choices that block the love experience, constantly sabotage it, or make it next to impossible for it to thrive.

My client Audra (not her real name) was never lonely. After her divorce, she wanted a relationship and wondered when love would come into her life again (although she asserted to me that she could easily live without a man in her life). But what she could not live without were her 13 cats. These cats were her life, and as we went through our sessions she spoke of them as her family, or her "furkids." This was all great, but what she didn't realize is that by pouring all her love and time into the cats, she had closed herself off from real human interaction. Animal hoarding is oftentimes a sign of someone who has shut down his or her heart chakra and disconnected from the human love experience. Such people seek out only unconditional love and acceptance, which is very easily received through animals. Unconditional love is a beautiful thing, but it doesn't allow or encourage growth by exercising or expanding your light-energy source. Even if love is unrequited it has value, because through the experience, you engage with another soul, you feel pain, you process the pain, and you grow from the experience. You are allowing the love energy to flow through you as you give out love, and if you're open to it, the universe will always send it back to you. Well, Audra was not open, and her behavior precluded the nurturing of her human side *and* her energetic, spiritual side. I am a huge animal lover, but when I see someone collecting animals and lacking human connections, I begin to delve deep and excavate the wounds that created the lock down in the first place.

Of course, Audra had to be ready for this. As I prompted her to really look at her behavior, she began to understand that she would never find love again because she was not open to it. Although she was thinking about finding love again (it was always on her mind), and although she thought she was open and ready, the shield of felines she literally surrounded herself with did not allow anyone to get too close. We began to talk about her marriage and consequent divorce, and she had the courage to go into the dark spaces of her heart and heal the wounds that had been festering there for many years. Her marriage had been codependent and dysfunctional, and her husband had been a serial cheater, which she allowed for many years until one of his affairs turned out to be more than a passing fancy. She had she stopped caring years before, so she wasn't devastated when they divorced—or so she thought. Her obvious complacency was in fact a clear sign that she shut down long before the divorce. In fact she had started to shut down when he cheated while she was pregnant with their first daughter. She had many years of toxic energy stored in her heart chakra.

As a Lightworker she still felt a need to nurture and give love after the divorce, so she poured all her light energy into her beloved cats, but she was unable to receive any of the human love experience because her heart chakra had long since closed. Understanding this began a long healing process for Audra. Slowly she began to open up her heart to other people. Through different visualizations and exercises we gently began to crack open the windows of her heart and peek inside. This was such a huge step for her and she began a passage to healing.

My clients are not always willing to do this, because it is too scary or painful to peer into the place where all your pain resides, but in time they are eventually forced to do it (as what happened to me with my illness) or, hopefully, they come to the realization that they need to heal in order to stave off total meltdown.

Heartbreak: A Weighty Issue

Another symptom of a Lightworker who is closed off is excessive weight gain. Of course this is not the only reason for weight gain, but I find the majority of my Lightworker clients who simply cannot lose weight have a wounded heart chakra that is on the verge of closing up or has already done so. Empaths are extremely sensitive and tend to feel everything physically. They are very in tune with the energy that is connected to the physical. In fact, empaths tend to connect more with what is going on outside of their own energy than within. When they surround themselves with dysfunctional people and relationships, they tend feel the effects physically. To soothe the pain that comes from being so sensitive, they may partake in unhealthy eating habits or indulge in comfort foods. We have all heard of the cliché of the heartbroken girl who eats a pint of ice cream, crying, while watching *The Notebook*, because she is grieving a failed relationship. This picture is not a far cry from a true portrayal of an empathic Lightworker who is brokenhearted. Empaths who lack awareness will seek out physical comforts rather than deal with the real source(s) of their pain. It feels good temporarily, but all it does is mask the toxic energy of pain.

When my client Claudia came to me with concerns about her on-again, off-again boyfriend, Gill, she told me she wondered whether the reason he wouldn't commit was because she had a weight problem. She explained to me they had been seeing each other for four years but she just couldn't get him to the "next level." He would drop out of sight for weeks, only call her when he felt like it, and basically made her feel disposable. He would never commit to a relationship or introduce her to his friends. Privately I wondered why Claudia chose to stick around for four years of this. Surely she must be tired of waiting. She expressed she was getting impatient but it never entered her mind to move on; she simply wanted me to tell her when he would eventually "come around." The truth was that he was never going to "come around." Gill was emotionally unavailable, and Claudia (without consciously realizing it) was attracted to him *for that very reason.* She was a survivor of sexual abuse at the hands of her stepfather, and she closed off her heart chakra when she was a teen. She never dealt with the abuse and just buried her pain. She had never married because she always chose men who were physically or emotionally available. Some were married, some lived far away, some were commitment-phobes— there was always some obstacle. This was Claudia's way of putting her pain on her partner rather than dealing with it herself. This was her method of disconnecting, of coping.

However, I sensed that she was not ready to dig in deep and heal. The abuse was too painful to confront. I worked with her gently on some heart chakra cleansing, and each time we did she became very upset. It's not a good thing to release too much pain or toxicity at once because the sudden onslaught of emotions can be end up re-traumatizing the person. Forcing open the heart chakra is never a good idea. It has to be a slow and gradual process of gently and carefully cleansing and then balancing the entire chakra system. Healing must be approached as a journey through a dark tunnel with light at the end.

So instead of focusing on Gill and why he was unavailable, I gently guided her sessions in a different direction of self-awareness. I prayed that, one day, I'd be able to get her to a place where she could begin to look into her pain. We worked on a few exercises for empaths, which actually helped her lose some weight. But the weight wasn't the real problem, of course; it was just a symptom of her pain. The goal is always to bring healing, but some clients, like Claudia, are resistant; sometimes the best that can be achieved is to bring some awareness that they are harboring toxic energy and that their pain is buried under the weight (or the addiction, or the hyper-focus on children, or whatever it is that they are choosing to mask it with).

Abandonment Issues: Lonely for Life?

Another issue for Lightworkers is getting past abandonment issues. When a Lightworker is abandoned as a child, whether physically or emotionally, it can set off a lifetime of feeling unworthy and isolated. My client Bill was given up when he was three years old. His mother was addicted to drugs and felt the best thing to do was to give up her two sons. It had been an open adoption, so Bill remained in touch with his birth mother throughout his life, mostly by phone as she lived in another state. Even though they spoke on the phone regularly, he felt such a void for maternal energy in his life. He felt abandoned by his mother and on a soul level questioned his self-worth. Wasn't he enough to make her quit the drugs? Perhaps she didn't love him, and that's why she gave him away.

Eventually the unprocessed pain of his wounded inner child contaminated his adult life and sabotaged all his relationships. He constantly sought out women who took him for granted, abused his kind soul, and then broke up with him. As hard as Bill tried to be a good man, he always ended up alone. The human ego is very clever in that it always seeks to validate fears. Bill consistently attracted women who would further prove that his damaged view of himself was accurate. The thing was, Bill was not connecting with these women at all; he was connecting with his wounds. He had disconnected from others a long time ago. He was on a quest his entire life to repeat the scenario he lived through as a child—maybe one day it would be different and he would not be abandoned. Maybe one day he would finally be good enough. This would never happen until Bill connected with another person and stopped allowing himself to be driven by his pain. Bill was not aware his relationship problems were connected to his abandonment issues. Bill never realized he felt unworthy of love because he had been given up by his birth mother. However, even though his adoptive parents were loving and supportive, he still felt that he had been given away because he wasn't good enough, and this is what had shut down his heart chakra. Instead of seeking out loving and caring partners, he spent his whole life trying to prove his mother wrong.

In my sessions with Bill we discussed connecting with his inner child and healing the abandonment issues. These efforts brought up pain that Bill was unaware he had, but we slowly processed through the toxic energy and gently opened up his heart charka. As the healing took place, his heart filled with fluid, and healing light energy, and he learned to give and receive love in a healthy way.

How Do You Disconnect?

There are many ways Lightworkers disconnect to shield their hearts and not feel the pain anymore. Everyone has a different methodology of disconnection; the previous cases are just a few examples. Are you on the edge of closing off? Have you already? Even if you are in a relationship you can still be energetically disconnected. Simply being aware that you are disconnected or that you are in danger of shutting down is the first step to keeping your love channel open. This awareness is your first step to healing and being able to engage in healthy bonds with others. To that end, ask yourself the following questions:

+ Do you often feel needy or clingy when you have strong feelings for someone?

+ Do you feel a need to be constantly validated by others?

+ Do you often feel unloved no matter how many people want to love you?

+ Are you generally suspicious or distrusting of others?

+ Do you find the partners you seek are never fully present in your relationship?

+ Do you notice negative patterns in your relationships?

+ Do you attract wounded or dysfunctional partners?

+ Do you find yourself hoarding useless items or even pets?

+ Do you enjoy the company of your pets more than people?

If you answered yes to most of these questions, ask yourself the following for some insight into your pain:

+ Are there traumatic events in my past that I have difficulty facing?

+ What emotional pains from my past require healing?

+ What relationships have had the most influence over who I am today?

+ Where do I harbor the most bitterness or painful memories? Against whom?

+ What do I need to forgive myself, and others, for?

+ How can I begin to release toxic energy, move forward, and begin to love myself and others again?

It is never too soon to embark on a healing process. To help stave off complete meltdown (and potentially physical breakdown as well), here are some ways to prepare yourself for the journey ahead:

+ Mediation and deep thought.

+ Connecting and listening to your higher self.

+ Changing your inner dialogue from being fearful to being loving and supportive.

+ Being kind to yourself and treating yourself as a valued part of the collective.

+ Mindful exercise.

+ Following a "clean" diet.

+ Practicing gratitude and reminding yourself daily of how precious the gifts of life and love are.

+ Feeling the protection and support from the higher spiritual realms.

Next we will discuss will eventually happen when an empathetic Lightworker does not take stock of his or her love energy. This is a place you do not want to find yourself in: the Lightworker meltdown.

CHAPTER 11

The Spiritual and Physical Meltdown

I f you have reached this stage it is now time to sound the alarm and get moving on getting your energy back to a healthy state. There comes a time when if you do not open up and cleanse your heart chakra, you will enter into this state I call meltdown. Although it can seem to hit you suddenly, it actually happens gradually over time. A Lightworker's love energy, which flows through the heart chakra, is literally your life source; the fourth chakra must be open and receptive to receiving love in order for

you to survive and thrive. If we shut down and remain this way for years at a time, it will adversely
affect our very foundation—emotional, physical,
and spiritual. Eventually, just like the boarded-up
house, your physical body will begin to break down.
A Lightworker with an unhealthy physical body
cannot complete her divine mission. Everything will
be unbalanced if the love energy of the universe is
blocked. This is why it is so important for you to remain ever mindful that the human love experience
(although sometimes painful) is meant to expand
your light energy not shut it out.

Isolation

Energetic isolation is a symptom of impending
meltdown. This is when you disconnect your energetic flow from others. This is a very unnatural state
of being, because we all share a divine connection.
Shutting off your line to the universe leaves you in
the dark. It's like shutting down the circuit breaker
to your home's electrical panel. The energy is still
there to make light, but you have shut off the connection so you have no choice but to live in darkness. Isolation for a Lightworker doesn't mean you
have to be physically alone. Even if you are in a relationship, surround yourself with family or friends,
or actively contribute to the GNP every day, you
may still be closed off without realizing it. Isolation
for a Lightworker occurs when you are not receptive to love, and your healing abilities are cut off.
This isolation can manifest itself in several ways,

including staying in dysfunctional or abusive relationships, remaining silent in your suffering, or expecting to live a life of unhappiness. All are signs that you have cut yourself off from your authentic love source. A Lightworker in isolation is clearly in "protection mode."

The spirit and the human counterpart need human interaction to thrive and grow. But if you do not process your pain, you may develop energetic scar tissue that is blocking the healthy flow of energy. Every human interaction has a purpose and presents an opportunity for growth. Shutting down and isolating only creates stagnation and in turn brings feelings of depression, sadness, and worthlessness. Although your ego is doing its best to protect your precious gifts (albeit misguidedly), you will find no solace in this protection, only loneliness and sadness. Because your heart chakra is where your life purpose is housed and fueled, if it is closed off in isolation, all aspects of your life will suffer. This is when the meltdown occurs.

Anatomy of a Meltdown

How a Lightworker melts down is as individual as each person's mission on earth. Some Lightworkers self-medicate and become addicted; some hoard or hold onto items or pets, desperately trying to fill the void; others become workaholics to avoid human connection. All of these behaviors distract from the pain and attempt to soothe the gnawing emptiness. Your spirit will do anything to protect its most sacred conduit, and if that means not engaging in relationships at all, so be it. However, you will still need to combat the human ego, which constantly seeks to assuage its fears. When the spirit shuts down, the ego steps up to fill the vacuum. Its goals are to feel good, avoid pain, and protect itself, all at the cost of actually living life to the fullest.

The problem is that ego simply cannot go without validation. This is because it only understands its own mortality and temporary physical existence. The human ego is fearful of rejection, fearful of not being good enough, fearful of ceasing to exist. Ego will send you on a wild goose chase to be validated by the human love experience. This brings into play all the pain and all the triggers that come from living. Relationships are no longer a sacred spiritual encounter; instead they become the arena where we battle all our darkest fears and human pain. There is no way we can achieve happiness in relationships when all we are doing is battling fear. Although we may start out with the intention of finding happiness, it will never come to us because we are functioning from a place of fear—meltdown—rather than authentic love. Shutting down our heart chakra cuts off all our resources to connect with the authentic forms of love, the universal love energy and other vibrational types we discussed.

So the end result is that we begin to accumulate more fear and more pain until we eventually collapse, both spiritually and physically. This meltdown occurs when we have allowed ourselves to be purely ego-driven for an extended period of time.

Depending on your native resolve and tenacity, this can take a long time or happen very quickly. But it is a foregone conclusion that a Lightworker who remains in a place of fear *will* melt down. Here are some symptoms of meltdown for a Lightworker:

You've begun to isolate yourself from others, even those you love most.

You've lost interest in making the world a better place.

You focus on the negative elements of society instead of the inspirational, uplifting events.

Your dreams for a better life are now seen as silly fantasies.

You hoard useless items or animals to fill the void created from a lack of light energy.

You do not honor your physical body (e.g., poor diet, unhealthy habits, lack of exercise, etc.).

You feel powerless in most situations.

You've become complacent.

You feel like you have lost the will to fight for your higher purpose.

You feel you will never find love.

You've lost faith in humanity.

You no longer can see the good in others.

You have become suspicious and distrustful.

You feel insecure in all of your relationships.

You would rather be with your pets than interact with people.

You've developed an addiction(s).

You battle with feelings of hopelessness.

What Is a Meltdown?

A meltdown can be emotional, physical, spiritual, or some combination thereof. It occurs when you have reached the point of total dysfunction in your relationships. A meltdown is a total disconnect from others on an energetic level. This means no sharing of light energy, no healing of others, and no expansion of your light energy. For a Lightworker this can be a dangerous position. As you shut down your connection to the universal love energy, you shut down your connection to the divine as well. This blocks access all the guidance and support from the universe that you need to assist you through life. Your intuition, your awareness, and your clarity of thought are all muddied by toxic energy.

Mental and/or physical ailments may find you eventually, as well. If the energy you thrive on as an energetic being is taken from you, you will wither away. When a Lightworker enters the meltdown stage, it can be difficult for her to find her way out. Many Lightworkers feel utterly hopeless or lost when they get to this point. Their wounds are continually compounded by the ego's quest to soothe its fears, and damage is piled on top of damage. With the heart chakra closed up, the other chakras begin to take the brunt of the toxic energy. Often your weakest points are where you will feel the effects of your meltdown. For example if you suffered sexual abuse, your second chakra is already vulnerable. During a meltdown you may begin to take on toxic energy in this chakra and experience health issues in the organs associated with that particular chakra—for example, fertility issues, sexual dysfunction, and problems with your reproductive organs.

If you look honestly at your behaviors, you will see a pattern of repeatedly seeking validation to fill a void. Abandonment issues, self-esteem issues, addictive behaviors—all of these stem from the fear-driven ego and overtake our ability to heal and be healed through love. Fear-driven relationships are often abusive, one-sided, or codependent, among other unhealthy characteristics. If you are in an unhappy relationship, ask yourself the following questions:

- ✦ In this relationship, do the same issues always arise without any resolution?
- ✦ Do I hold resentment or hostility toward this person?
- ✦ Do I sometimes feel this person does not support my greatest good?
- ✦ Does this relationship enhance my life?
- ✦ Do a lot of my relationships seem stagnant or feel as though they are going nowhere?
- ✦ Do I often feel devalued by my partner?
- ✦ Am I often insecure with or jealous of my partner?
- ✦ Do I find myself repeatedly going back to partners who hurt me deeply?

If you answered mostly yes to these questions, you are likely in an ego-supported, fear-driven relationship, and meltdown may be just around the corner.

The Way Out

Sadly, many Lightworkers get lost in meltdown and can never find their way out again This is so unnecessary, as there is always hope. You have the love and support of your guides to draw on, and teachers of the higher realms who are accessible to you at all times. The best way out is to simply be open to dialoging with your guides and teachers in the higher realms who will guide you out of the meltdown phase. This is as easy as asking for help, with the knowledge that help *will* be delivered: Ask and you shall receive.

Many Lightworkers find themselves stuck waiting for a partner to return. They can go years and years waiting for a long lost love to return, in order to make amends or reconcile. They become so focused on healing fear that they actually create or conjure it within themselves. As empaths we tend to see everyone as a mirror of ourselves. Could it be that it is the Lightworker who is afraid to connect and is projecting these fears onto someone who has no idea they are the poster child for their own fear of real connection? If you find yourself in a similar situation, always chasing the unattainable, living in the past, or focusing on someone who has given you no indication that he or she desires to be in a relationship with you, it is time to examine your inner core and find the true motivating source of your behavior. Let's look in our own mirror and ask the frightening question: What am I afraid of? The answer is usually simple, although the solution is not. Because usually at this point the heart chakra has been shut down or is so guarded that it cannot connect in an authentic way with others. Instead the ego steps forward points a finger outwardly; and excuses you from doing the internal work needed to move forward with healthy connections.

When I work with my clients I can often hear or feel the frustration of their guides in the spirit world when the client is resistant to their help. If this is the case I ask the client to explore whether he or she is really asking for help or merely saying the words. Opening up your channel to divine guidance is an important first step. This opens you up to hope and shifting your perspective that you are never alone in your suffering. Remember: You do not need to do anything to change the situation or situations that are causing you pain right now; you only need to shift your perspective. Seeing the glass as half full rather than half empty is a good example. Awareness that you have the control to change your view and process the pain that has foisted you into the dark is so empowering. As a Lightworker you will never be left in the dark by those who have assisted you since day one in your journey. You were not brought here to fail in your mission! The wise ones of the higher realms would not have put this higher calling within you if they weren't going to empower you with the tools you need to succeed.

With all this mind, we can see the meltdown phase as a learning experience rather than as simply a negative situation, but only if we are willing to process the pain to the point of clawing our way out and getting back on the track to our divine mission. If and when the meltdown comes, call out to your support system within the divine hierarchy of the universe. These are your teachers and spirit guides, the angels and ascended masters, and, always, your source creator. They will lift you out of the dark place of your meltdown and deliver you to a place of glorious love and light, healing your wounds and clearing your divine healing channel for love.

In the next chapter of this book, we are going to dig deep and find out how you may have gotten to this phase and how to work your way out. We will go as far back as childhood, where the parental relationship sets the stage for all future relationships. When a Lightworker child does not have the proper foundation or springboard from which to use the inherent gifts he was born with to fulfill his mission, all other interactions can be affected. We will discuss how to examine your spirit and your chakras, and exorcise the ghosts of the past and process them back to the original light energy with which you came into this world. This journey through soul wounds and out of the darkness can be difficult, but in order to find love and balanced relationships, it needs to be done. Consider it a "love energy detox." Get ready to shift your perspective!

CHAPTER 12

Excavating Soul Wounds

As I mentioned in the previous chapter, once you have reached this meltdown phase and cut yourself off from your love source, it can be a difficult journey out of the darkness. It is an often arduous journey to seek and find the road out of darkness, but it is a glorious path to self-discovery. Once you are ready to excavate your soul wounds and dig out pain that you thought was long dead and buried, you will unearth the ghosts of your past. The reason these ghosts still reside within you is because you may have found it too difficult or inconvenient to deal with them. But that changes now! Your energy channels are like clogged drains and pipes, which will eventually back up. In order to avoid this, you need to clear away the offending clog. Imagine the ugly stuff that you will dredge up. This is kind of like what excavating your soul wounds will feel like: yucky, but a huge relief when it's done. In order to clear out all the muck and mire that has you blocked, first we need to get to the core of where it all came from, the source of the clog, as it were. So let's start at the beginning.

The Sources of Our Wounds

When we are born into this human existence we are born into community. We begin interacting with others almost from day one. The maternal bond is the first of these interactions, and it must be strong for an infant to survive and thrive. Studies have shown that babies that do not experience that powerful bonding experience do not gain as much weight, do not reach milestones in a timely manner, and oftentimes do not thrive in the same manner as babies that have a powerful maternal bond. As we grow and mature, our experiences as we relate to others take their effects on us, both positive and negative. As Lightworkers and energetic beings, we also begin to absorb the energies of these interactions. These energies can be light, dark, or anywhere in between. To a sensitive Lightworker or empathic child, these energies can have a powerful impact.

When we are wounded by someone, toxic energy is immediately created and stored. We are presented with a choice: Can either "flush out" the wound with light energy and heal it; or we can hold onto it, allowing it to fester and grow. If we harbor toxic energy from wounds, it will anchor itself firmly in one of our chakras, ultimately creating all kinds of problems. As we hold onto this dark energy (which converts into pain), the Law of Attraction kicks in, and we begin to attract more dark energy. It may take years until we see the effects manifest themselves in our adult relationships. The manifestation will be dysfunction, energetic blocks, and behavioral patterns that bring us back to a state of unhappiness, almost replaying how the pain originated in the first place. We need to peel away layers upon layers of toxic energy to get to the source of our pain, the start of it all.

When we don't process pain, our heart chakra shuts down, and the love energy channels through an inappropriate passage, usually another chakra. When this happens, the toxic energy will re-route itself to the surface and spread throughout our entire existence. Eventually we are affected to the point that we find ourselves repeatedly dealing with the same relationship issues. This, coupled with the Lightworker's propensity to give and give until they have nothing left, leaves us emotionally, physically, and spiritually drained. Vulnerable. Empty. Healing our pain is the key to channeling the different types of love energies properly and keeping our energetic passageways clear. Many times we need healing for pain that we do not even recognize we are carrying. Regardless, it's imperative to start with the underlying causes first before we can move forward into healthy relationships.

Sometimes a sensitive Lightworker or (empathetic) person will hold onto her pain to such an extent that it becomes a part of herself. There is no more separation: Self equates to pain and vice versa. If this is you, know that holding onto pain will transform you fundamentally and actually alter your perception of reality. The anxious attachment relationship you have with your pain creates a fear of letting go and generates an immediate resistance to release. It's almost like saying good bye to someone who has been a part of your life for so long you can't imagine your life without him or her. In this way, releasing and letting go of your pain is similar to a death. You may grieve your pain, not understand life without it, or feel totally alone. Letting go, even of something negative, always involves a sense of loss. If you think about it, it makes sense: Our pain creates fear energy, and fear is something that keeps us safe. Without the fear energy, we feel vulnerable, lacking the protective shield we have become so dependent on. This is all an illusion, though, as it is a false sense of security. Because our fears in this case do not protect us, but only stop us from pursuing happiness and mastery of our Lightworker role.

The Lightworker path is one of ascension and expansion of light energy. When we remain stagnant, we diminish our light energy. When our light energy is not expanding, we begin to spiral downward and attract the same type of stagnant, underdeveloped energy we are carrying with us. This will manifest as toxic, dysfunctional, and self-destructive behavior patterns and relationships.

Identifying Our Wounds

This world is a harsh place, and a person who is highly empathetic and sensitive is affected by emotional pain even more than the average sentient being. Pain from abuse, abandonment, and toxic people or environments can leave us with wounds. Pain is a very personal and individual experience. Combine the Lightworker's sensitivity with negative life experiences and the thoughtless or malicious actions of others, and the perfect storm is created to wound your spirit. It makes no difference whether the wound is created by a small incident or a huge trauma—it still transforms into the same energetic vibration that creates our spiritual wounds. The sooner you begin to address your pain, honor it, and begin the process of releasing it, the faster you will begin the healing journey.

Discovering your pain

Let's say you know are you feeling sad, isolated, or alone, all sure indications that you are in pain on some level. You will need to identify the underlying source or sources of your pain. Consider the following questions as you explore where your pain might have come from:

✦ When or how did it originate?

+ Where are you harboring it in your energy?
+ In what ways is it manifesting itself in your life?

Use these questions as springboards to your exploration. (As I mentioned earlier in the book, if your trauma was severe, you may need to do this within the safe confines of a therapist's office.) Once you identify your pain, you'll need to take full ownership of it. No longer can you blame others for inflicting it upon you or constantly rehash what happened. You now own this pain and it is yours to handle. For now, leave the forgiveness for those who hurt you for later. Just know that once you have transformed the pain, you will not only have immediate forgiveness, but you will actually feel gratitude toward the other person for helping you grow. Just beginning by taking ownership empowers you and takes away the victim mentality.

Getting in touch with your pain

Meditation is a simple and easy way to get insight as to what is going on with your energy. Set aside a few minutes each day to remain in stillness and silence and ask for guidance. Start by asking your higher self, guides, angels, God, whoever it is that resonates with your spirit, **"Please help me feel my pain and fill me with healing light."** Notice the wording. You are asking to *feel* your pain. As you ask this question in meditation you may begin to feel certain sensations. Be aware of any slight tingle, feeling, warm sensation, or perhaps even actual physical pain. (Don't worry, your spirit will be gentle; any excessive pain will be your human side stepping in to stop the process. Honor this.) Notice where this feeling is in your physical body, and try to be so present in the moment. As you feel your pain, recall as many details as you can about the sensation.

It is also important to take note of any visions, words, or phrases that come to mind during this practice. They will have significant meaning for you. Stand up to your discomfort and allow it to linger until it subsides; unless the physical pain becomes too much, do not shut down and run from it. Remember it is time to heal and open up, not shut down. It's all part of the healing process. Just by recognizing and honoring your pain, you are automatically flushing it out with white light and engaging in the healing process.

The location of pain

During this exercise, it is also important to note *where* you are feeling sensations, because this will indicate to you where your wound is festering. Let's go over the chakras and learn what sensations in each could possibly indicate:

+ **Root chakra** at the base of your spine: Could indicate a fear or wound stemming from abandonment, or a fear of not having the essentials for survival. Perhaps in your childhood you felt physically unsafe. Sensation or discomfort in this area indicates that you do not feel safe in the physical world.

+ **Sacral chakra** below the navel: Sensation in this area could indicate sexual issues or, at worst, sexual abuse. Perhaps you were wounded during a mutually consensual sexual encounter.

+ **Solar plexus chakra** above the navel and below the heart: Sensation here indicates control and trust issues. Perhaps you were in a painful situation in which you had no control and now do not trust others or even yourself.

+ **Heart chakra** at the center of the chest: Sensation here indicates lack of empathy or unconditional love from others in your life. The human ego is harmed from interactions that have to do with love and human bonds.

+ **Throat chakra** in the hollow of your neck or throat: Sensations in this area mean you have been prevented from expressing your emotions. Articulation, communication, and emoting have been blocked by relationships or situations in your life.

+ **Third eye chakra** in the center of the forehead, above the eyebrow: You may have been denied the power of your intuition. This could have occurred because people did not honor your strengths and insights. You may have felt insignificant to those around you, and you may live in a fantasy world to escape the pain of being dismissed by those you hold most dear.

✦ **Crown chakra** at the top of the head: Sensation here can mean that painful events in your life have caused you to lose your faith. This could occur by being let down by those we look to for guidance (parents are a prime example). Perhaps your parents were neglectful or did not show their love for you in a manner that helped nurture your growth toward becoming an adult who feels validated and valued. Our mothers and fathers represent the love of God. If we do not feel this powerful type of love, we lose our faith and close off our channel to the divine.

These explanations are generalizations. Everyone has their own variation and story behind their wounds, but this will give you a good start as to what to look for and what to further explore when attempting to identify where you are holding your pain and where your toxic energy found its way into your essence. Once you discover your story or journey to pain, you will reveal the true origin of your energetic wounds.

The next step is to cleanse the area and release the toxic energy stored there. Perhaps you can easily identify where the pain is and how it originated, and that is wonderful, because it gives you a starting point. You may discover your toxic energy in a particularly weak point in your body. Here are some very general examples:

+ Root chakra: lower back issues.
+ Second chakra: issues with reproductive organs.
+ Third chakra: stomach and digestive issues.
+ Fourth chakra: cardiovascular issues, heart palpitations.
+ Fifth chakra: throat issues
+ Sixth chakra: mental health issues, depression, anxiety.
+ Seventh chakra: Alzheimer's or dementia.

Recognition and awareness that you are actually in pain is the very first step toward releasing the pain and putting a stop to any physical issues that may occur. As noted, everyone is different, so as the saying goes, your mileage may vary.

Cleansing and releasing

Moving forward, once we identify where we are holding our pain, we need to cleanse this area and remove the toxic energy that is feeding our wounds. Visualization is a wonderful start to cleansing. Water is an amazingly healing element that I use in visualization. Here's how to cleanse and release: Envision the chakra at issue being cleansed with crystal-clear water and then being filled with healing, white light. You can maximize the effects by doing this in a bathtub or shower. Spend extra time allowing the water to pour over the area in question, as you envision healing light filling the area.

It is important to conduct this cleansing on all seven chakras weekly in order to keep your energy balanced and all your chakras cleansed. As you continue to practice this literal cleansing, you are releasing pain energy. Be careful not to release too much at a time. If you begin to feel overwhelmed with emotion or unpleasant feelings, it's time to stop for that day. You can try again the next day, releasing the pain energy a little at a time. Remember: Healing is a journey, not a destination. You will get there, but the journey is where you will discover all your spiritual gifts and how you buried them under pain for so deep and for so long. So take your time, and use the healing path as a path to self-discovery as well.

✦

PART IV

✦

PART IV.

CHAPTER 13

Rediscovering Our Authentic Self

O nce we heal our wounds and separate ourselves from our fears, what are we left with? This is a scary question for some of us. Under all the layers of pain and toxic energy is a pure being, the authentic *you* who kind of got lost long ago. You sacrificed your authentic self in relationships to please others and eventually lost touch with your greatest ally. What really is the authentic self, though, and how do you really know how to identify it? The authentic self clearly emerges when you come to a place of peace and ease with yourself and others around you. There really is no mistaking it once you have it. When you get down to your authentic core you no longer feel that you are responsible for other people's happiness, nor are they responsible for yours.

You will find the self that you forgot existed, the *you* that you must now rediscover and celebrate. This is a glorious time for many Lightworkers. They have finally realized who they are apart from the human experience and now recognize themselves as spiritual beings who have a divine purpose. Our own authenticity is as individual as a fingerprint. None of us are exactly alike, and we aren't measured according to any yardstick imposed by others or their purposes. Finally discovering who we are under all the pain is the greatest gift of all in this entire process of love and creating human bonds. Until we truly know and love ourselves unconditionally, we cannot love another without expectations or fear.

Change Is Good

Once you clear yourself of all your toxic energy you will discover a fundamental change in the way you view life and your relationships. You will discover that relationships are beautiful again, and you will value yourself enough to practice love equitably, even if that means walking away when you are giving too much and not receiving love in return. When you practice authenticity in your life, you will:

✦ No longer feel the need to change to please others;

✦ Not have a problem saying no with kindness;

✦ Live your life on your terms, not those dictated by others or by society;

✦ Have a clearly defined sense of who you are;

✦ Live the purpose-driven life of your choice;

✦ Believe in yourself like never before;

✦ Take responsibility for your own happiness;

✦ Not enable others with the hidden agenda to validate yourself;

✦ Be bold enough to follow your dreams without reservation; and

✦ Accept life's challenges as a loving and generous opportunity from the universe to grow exponentially.

All these changes are a result of living in authenticity. But that's not all: There are more exciting and wonderful things in store for you as well!

The Authentic Path to Love

Moving forward, once you are on the healing path, your heart chakra will open up and be able to maintain your light energy. Because of this you will experience a huge shift in relationships. You will no longer take on a victim or enabler role, but the role of a supportive and loving partner in the journey through life. Expectations will also be removed, and you will allow relationships to grow organically into something beautiful. Conversely, if your partner is not in alignment with you, you will have the courage to walk away freely and without resentment. You will seek an equal partner who is living authentically as well. Together you will create a bond that will be more powerful than any other you have experienced because it originated from a place of wholeness and authenticity.

Travel baggage free

Free from all the baggage from the past you will love and connect in a new light. Now you will be able to engage others from a place of empowerment and love, instead of fear and pain. Finding that authentic place where ego is cast aside and spirit steps in is like chains being removed your entire life and being illuminated with ultimate truth. This illumination will allow you to finally find balance in love. The spirit knows no fear and understands that we are all one; there is no such thing as pain or separation where love exists. Fear-based relationships or counterproductive energies are all but eliminated. Jealousy, possessiveness, insecurity, and trust issues are all based on fear of loss. Of course no one wants to lose their romantic partner; these human emotions are real and natural. But to live your life carrying the constant weight of the fear what *could* happen is not living true to yourself.

Some people get into relationships just to say they are in one. Not surprising, considering how important it is in this culture to be in a relationship. Just look at social media. A friend will proudly change his "status" to "in a relationship," and everyone offers their congratulations and well wishes. A change in relationship status is a nice time to offer well wishes, but why not offer well wishes to your friend just for being him. We celebrate coupling as though it is the be all, end all, as though the people involved just won a one-way ticket on the happiness train. In most cases it doesn't always turn out that way, especially when someone judges his or her value depending on his or her relationship status. This need for adoration or applause on a public forum screams of insecurity and fear. Perhaps this sounds a bit harsh, but let me ask this: Does this type of declaration really enhance the person at the core level, or is it just boosting the ego? This is when we need to reexamine what truly defines us and what is just egocentric, fear-based, extraneous stuff.

Your authentic self will have a keen sense of when you are falling into a fearful or insecure place in your relationships, when you are functioning on a lower vibratory level that is nothing but ego driven. But when you are fearless and love beyond the limitation of human attachments, you will discover you have absolutely nothing to fear, because true love energy is infinite. Also you will no longer be held hostage by your human fear-driven self in relationships. Your ability to love will expand, and you will love without limitations or attachment to outcomes. Trying to force or leverage outcomes that we think will validate us will lead to disaster—for example, fearing that if we don't marry by a certain age we will be looked upon negatively. This type of fear often leads us to choose the wrong partner just because we want to force what we think is expected of us.

Another benefit is that Lightworkers who tend to fall into total selflessness when it comes to loving others will become more self-aware. Being completely selfless is crossing a clear line between healing with love and taking on the responsibility for someone else's wounds. Lightworkers *cannot* heal those who do not want to face their pain. Just as you had to come to the place of being willing to let go of your pain, others need to be ready as well. Our stubborn nature to heal sometimes becomes a liability when it comes to our own personal relationships.

Unhealthy Selflessness

As I already mentioned, Lightworkers are here to give of their healing light, but they must carefully honor their own needs as well. Here are some questions to ask yourself if you think your healing nature may be interfering in your authentic path and your love life. If you agree with more than half of these questions, it is time to readjust your approach to love.

+ I usually choose partners who have addictive personalities.
+ I make excuses for my partner's shortcomings.
+ I am often told that I am controlling.

✦ My partner feels I am smothering at times.

✦ I cover (or lie) to keep my partner from experiencing humiliation or consequences.

✦ I think my partner's friends are a bad influence.

✦ I often give my partner sound advice that he/she never follows.

✦ I often excuse my partner for bad behavior because I feel he/she is afraid to love.

✦ I will wait for my partner to "fix" his/her life and help him/her to recover.

✦ I excuse my partner for not committing to me it because he/she has been hurt in previous relationships.

If you are allowing any of these situations to linger for a sustained period of time, you are attempting to heal someone rather than be engaged in an equal and balanced relationship. This is the primary tension and dichotomy for all Lightworkers. Discovering this will also awaken you to your authentic self as a human being who needs to give and receive love with balance.

Regaining Balance

When we are finally in touch with our authenticity, the divine balance of healer and human will take its rightful place in your life, and you will realize when you are being depleted and not receiving authentic love energy in return. You will discover that the universe is always in perfect balance. For every situation that seems unfair or unwarranted, the universe creates an equal and opposite situation to balance it out. For example, if there is war, the universe *has* a solution for peace; if there is famine, there *is* a way to provide food to the hungry; if there is a disease, rest assured the universe *has* already provided a cure—we just need to discover it. Just as happens in your experiences in love and human interactions, if you have the awareness and temerity to search for solutions, you will find the best ones, the ones that bring everything back into perfect balance again. Balance is a Lightworker's greatest friend!

Who Are You, Anyway?

Your authentic self is the spirit found at your absolute core, under all the "stuff" we have discussed. It is the part of you not defined by your human identity, and goes way deeper than that. It is all that your spirit embodies and feels compelled to embrace. True authenticity is not dictated by social or cultural ideals, mores, or standards. You will discover you are not your pain, you are not what people told you that you are, you are not what society tells you to be: You are a spiritual being with a divine purpose, and you have the power to heal yourself and the planet. As you release the constraints of the human identity and all the pain and toxicity that go with it, you will find that long ago, you forgot who you were. When this awakening comes for you, you will free yourself from cultural or societal identities— mother, husband, friend, gay, straight, victim, loser, whatever—and discover a uniquely divine being created by God put here to assist humanity. This is the purpose of the person who works in the light.

The footpath to self-discovery is not an easy passage. Getting to that place of authenticity is an awakening and takes some time to adjust to. How do you recognize yourself after all this time? Many clients come to me with the question: What is my life purpose? What am I supposed to be doing, and why was I put here on the planet at this time? All these questions reveal a search for their authentic self. My answer is always simple: Follow what resonates with you. Once you awaken, your life will change, and your priorities will be restructured. Eventually you will hear a subtle calling, and this will be your life purpose, your authentic self. Additionally, your intuition will be restored and heightened; once again you will feel the confidence to follow this inner voice. This simple ability to listen and feel will undoubtedly guide you to your ultimate life purpose and who you are at your core.

How empowering is it to release yourself from pain and become a warrior of the light? There is no nobler role to embrace as a human being.

CHAPTER 14

Returning to Love Begins With "I Am"

As we clear and cleanse our heart chakra and it begins to open up, we will return to a healthy energetic state. Now the love energy will channel through properly, and your healing properties will be restored. You will be able to return to a place where you can connect to and love others. But something else even more miraculous will also take place: You will be able to love yourself once again. That's what the journey you have been on was all about, not to find romance, get more dates, or even find a husband or wife. The journey I outline in this book is a journey to love, self-love.

When you closed off long ago, your heart chakra didn't discriminate when it came to deciding whom to block out. Along with blocking others, you probably also blocked your ability to love yourself. Self-love is where we all begin as human beings. A baby considers itself the center of the universe and seeks only to have its own needs met. Babies are all about themselves! They truly practice self-love by making sure their needs are met first; if they are not, they demand it in the most adorably insistent of ways. They also instinctively know that they will thrive on loving human interaction, and they will uninhibitedly seek this out as well. They need human love to thrive and you can see the comfort they take from it in their reactions. What brilliant and self-aware little beings they are! We all began in this place of ultimate self-love.

As we grow into awareness we are more or less forced into adaptation of social, cultural, and familial ideals. The growing child now shifts its focus to others and changes to seek validation from the outside world: "If you don't pick up your toys, Mommy will not read you a bedtime story" or "If you're not a good boy, you cannot have the candy you're asking for." All these types of behavior modifications create a new void, a need to be validated by others. These demand/reward interactions take away the self-awareness and self-validation we are born with, creating a false sense of identity by producing a need to please others. This is one way we begin to form our opinion of ourselves through the eyes of others. If we disappoint, we feel devalued. As time goes by we lose touch with that beautiful innate sense of self-awareness. We seek to find love externally and forget about what's needed internally. Lightworkers in particular tend to lose touch with their own needs as they tirelessly seek to fill the needs of others. This does not honor their journey. This will eventually cause them to lose that sense of "I am."

Redefining "I Am"

As we grow into adulthood the "I am" inside us continues to seek out love and validation from others. This sets us up to be victimized by others who do not honor our journey. We begin to take on the identity assigned to us by others or society in general. This will usually eviscerate any sense of authentic self we were born with. What begins to follow the "I am" are empty spiritually inauthentic labels: I am a good girl, I am a straight-A student, I am a stay-at-home mom, I am a secretary, I am a police officer, and so on. The list can go on and on with labels. Even *I am a Lightworker* can be considered a label. There is nothing inherently wrong with labels; in fact, they can be a source of pride, but we must also not forget that there is so much more to us than the labels we wear. Labels usually don't speak to what is the fundamental authentic self, but to how society puts a value on us.

Those who are labeled similarly are all different. We are much, much more than the labels foisted on us or the ones we put on ourselves. The words that follow "I am" are very powerful. We seek to be defined somehow, as if without a label we are pointlessly and detachedly living without a purpose. Without them, we feel out of alignment with others. If we dig deeper, however, we know that we are much more than any descriptor or label. Carefully putting in place the words that resonate in your heart after "I am" will tell you so much about yourself. Try to follow "I am" with words that resonate with your energy rather than with your human identity. Here are some examples:

+ I am vibrant.
+ I am grateful.
+ I am powerful.
+ I am inspired.
+ I am dreary.
+ I am dim.
+ I am dark.

Taking away occupations or social roles and replacing them with energetic terms or emotional expressions will tell you so much about who you are at this time and place in your life. Doing this also shows you that you have the power to transform yourself at any time. We are never stuck with a label given to us or even one that we have claimed for ourselves. What a hopeful position to be in, to know that we can control what comes after "I am"! We are no longer defined by our job, our status, our mistakes, or even our achievements. You are now defined *by yourself* as a unique, ever-evolving spirit, because your energetic self is your true and authentic self.

Of course the words you follow "I am" with will change and transform over time, just as your energy will. Today this word choice or phrase is just a snapshot in time, like a Polaroid. After the snapshot, things move forward and naturally metamorphose into another moment in time. In what direction you move forward in the next snapshot depends on how you move your energy and your state of being. If the words that resonate with you after "I am" are not reflecting a state of bliss, you have the power to change this.

I Am Loved: Ways to Practice Self-Love

Now we have opened our hearts and worked to define ourselves as more than just a product of our family, culture, or society, we can come to a place of truly knowing and loving ourselves again. This is the true return to love. It's not jumping back into the dating pool or joining an online dating service or even meeting a soulmate. The path back to love begins with the love of who I am. Here are some helpful practices for self-love:

1. **Release all guilt.** Many times Lightworkers harbor so much guilt when loving themselves. They feel selfish when they do this. There is such an inner need to be of service that some do not feel entitled to personal happiness. This may not be expressed outwardly

or even be a conscious thought, but it is of
their nature that they want to give of their
gifts. Limits need to be set or you will risk
falling into a trap of self-destruction. So,
Lightworker, do not feel guilty because you
gently said no or you drew a line in the sand!
This does not mean you're selfish; it means
you are honoring your own life. Guilt is a
dark emotion that can quickly overtake you.
Certainly it will not help you achieve mastery
of your Lightworker role.

2. **Set healthy boundaries with others.** When
engaging in relationships, know your limitations and set clear boundaries with others.
If you feel taken advantage of, communicate
this in a kind and loving way. There usually
is no need to disassociate yourself immediately or cut someone off forever if someone
oversteps boundaries. You can first lovingly
let the person know that you feel his behavior
is not in line with a healthy relationship and
that you would like to discuss how to bond
on a more mutually beneficial level. Others
who continuously overstep your boundaries may not be in alignment with your own
needs. If this is the case, love yourself enough
to walk away. There is nothing wrong with
helping a friend, but when you find you are
always drained or exhausted after being with
someone, it means she is needy beyond any
amount anyone can give. If, despite your kind
love and support, she will not do the work to

heal herself, then perhaps it's time for you to move on.

3. **Keep your inner dialogue kind.** A very important aspect of keeping self-love alive is your inner dialogue. When you dialogue with yourself, are you as kind and loving as you are with others? As an empath you can feel the pain of others, but do you consider your own pain when you engage in the internal dialogue process? Do you often tell yourself you will never find happiness or you are destined to be alone? These are all painful objectives you are inadvertently setting for yourself. This type of self-talk sets the stage for manifestation in your life. What you tell yourself is what you will perceive. Lightworkers can be kind and loving to others—why not show yourself the same compassion? Being ever mindful to stay positive, supportive, and loving when communicating internally is a big part of loving yourself! Constantly telling yourself how terrible your life is or how much of a failure you are will immediately impact your life as you perceive it. Conversely, focusing on your gifts and blessings will bring more goodness into your life and you will see miracles occur.

4. **Love your body.** As we have discussed, your journey is a glorious mixture of both the physical and spiritual world, and we must honor both. Our physical body is not just a vessel, but a gift to be honored and treated

with dignity. Learn to love and accept the skin you are in. Society has its ideals of physical beauty, but there is no truer statement than beauty is in the eye of the beholder. You are a masterpiece, a spark of the divine, so how could you be anything but beautiful? The measurements of physical beauty change as quickly as the tide, so don't allow society to force comparisons on you. Care for your physical body; nurture it with a healthy diet, mindful, exercise, and a lifestyle that keeps it as free from stress as possible.

5. **Celebrate your accomplishments, even the small ones.** Lightworkers are some of the most humble people I know. Humility is a noble trait, but there is nothing wrong with celebrating your accomplishments with others, no matter how small or insignificant they may seem. If you worked hard and feel you did the best you can, reward yourself. Honor your efforts with a good old-fashioned pat on the back. It's okay to feel and show pride for the good things you have done, the hard work you have engaged in, and the dreams you have fulfilled. If no one else celebrates you, celebrate yourself! Remember that you would do it for someone else.

6. **Embrace your shortcomings.** Isn't it a wonderful thing to be so perfect in your imperfections? Your shortcomings are not liabilities; they are inroads to understanding that you have a journey ahead of you to learn and

grow. There is no pressure to be perfect or compare yourself to those who appear to have achieved more than you have. Life is never short on rewards or blessings; there is enough for everyone. Be happy for others when they succeed, and see your shortcomings as your chance to grow. If we reached a limit on possibilities there would be nowhere to go from there and we would stop progressing. Your shortcomings are part of who you are and part of what makes you so unique.

7. **Don't ever give up on your dreams.** We all have dreams and aspirations. Many times we think, *It's too late for me. I missed my chance. I guess being a [writer, dancer, singer, etc.] is just not in the cards for me.* Well, I am here to tell you that it's never too late. I suffer from dyslexia. My entire life I was told I would never be a writer because I had a disability. Despite that, I knew that the desire to help others through writing was burning inside me. Although it was not easy, I never gave up on my dream. To my delight, spellcheck has become my best friend! All kidding aside, if you feel the desire to write a book, this means there is a book inside you waiting to come out. If you feel the desire to become an artist, that means that there is an artist inside you waiting to emerge and create. Don't give up; honor your dreams, because if you didn't have it in you to accomplish it, you would never have the desire to do it.

8. **Re-parent yourself if you need to.** Even the most well-meaning parents make mistakes. Hurtful words or thoughtless gestures can wound our inner child forever. Remember that this little wounded child still lives inside you and is disrupting your adult life. If you have parental wounds, whatever they may be, you now need to be a parent to this inner child and comfort him or her. This can be done through mediation and visualization. Envision this wounded child and telling him or her how cherished he or she is. You can go back in time and be the parent you wished you had. This brings tremendous healing and allows the inner child to feel the protection and nurturing that she never felt growing up in the physical reality.

Self-love is at the core of all the different love energies we discussed. It is your foundation for loving others and the first step to living a heart-centered existence. Without internal love, external love could never exist.

Conscious Awareness

Keeping your awareness raised at all times keeps you open to insightful guidance from the universe. When we are not in tune with ourselves we begin to shift our awareness onto the mundane, unimportant elements of our lives and become overly focused there. Stay focused and aware of your authentic self. You will find so much empowerment in the awareness of who you are and that you have a divine purpose. Do not ever lose sight of this. Awareness is a pathway to self-discovery. Keeping your senses sharp by being aware of the energies around you and how you are responding to them will help you stay centered. Exercises that work on the root chakra will keep you grounded in your earthly life and aware of when fear is beginning to creep in where it is not welcome. As you continue healing and mastering your role, toxic energy will leave your physical body and may cause you to feel ungrounded. Any shift in energy can feel a bit unsettling. Be aware of what it feels like to lose that precious balance, and refocus each time. Remember that this release is only bringing in healthy new light energy. Enjoy this wonderful transformation!

CHAPTER 15

Shifting Our Perspective: From Victim to Warrior

Empathy, sensitivity, and a need to bring healing are all fundamental parts of the Lightworker. These are gifts that we were given by our creator to heal the earth. At times we can overextend ourselves in personal relationships and the gifts, instead of being sources of love and light, become the very reasons for our personal unhappiness. Instead of Light warriors, working in the light to heal, we become victims of our own inclinations. Being a Light warrior does not mean being argumentative

183

or aggressive. It does not mean you will be at war with anyone. In fact, it is just the opposite. Being a Light warrior is a posture of love and peace, where no one is victimized and all intentions are for the greater good. It simply means never being victimized because of your generous nature.

Once our human self allows the victim mentality to anchor itself into our energy, it is very difficult to shake. However, there are life changes you can make to shake off this victim identity. You are a warrior of the light and must not allow anyone or anything to take this noble task from you by depleting your resources. Here are some characteristics of a Light warrior for you to contemplate. Understanding what being a warrior means will empower you to lose the victim identity and step into the powerful role you were destined to fulfill.

Authenticity

A Light warrior lives an authentic life, true to himself in every aspect. Authenticity means knowing yourself beyond your humanity, beyond your mortality, and in a place that is the infinite source of your core self. Authenticity is expressed in a life of substance that goes way beyond financial abundance or material success. An authentic Lightworker knows his purpose and is not afraid to reach a level of mastery. Authenticity is not politically correct, it is not conforming, and it is not how others perceive you. Authenticity is candidly being true to your spirit and making no apologies.

Once you familiarize yourself with your authenticity you will have the insight and clarity you need to know what is right for you. Along with this clarity will come the courage to take a brave stand. Authenticity is living endowed by what is true for you alone. When you live true to your authentic self, no one can *ever* victimize you. You will never allow the accusing voices of others (or yourself!) to shame you into not being who you truly are or not fulfilling your destiny. As you become powerful in this authenticity, you will fight for the authenticity of others, as well. *This* is a Light warrior.

Fearlessness

What does it mean to be fearless? First let's examine what fear really is. Fear is a defense mechanism put in place to help keep us safe. This emotion, as does any other, creates energy in your life. The physical world is a fearful place because we need to stay safe from bodily harm and protect our mortality. Fear has its rightful place if, for example, you decided to put your hand in a flame. The fear mechanism kicks in and says, *Don't do that; you're going to get hurt!* This is when fear is your friend, but when fear overtakes the spirit and your energy, it can be your biggest adversary.

Fear energy is heavy and dark, and will stop you from working in the light. Your authentic self cannot be harmed in the way that your mortality can. As we heal our wounds, fear begins to lift from our energy, and we feel light again. But when we allow fear to overtake our spirit, it becomes a controlling doomsday prepper who is constantly warning you that your demise is near. Fear looks at the lives of others and tells you that yours is not as good or that you could never achieve that kind of happiness, so don't even try. It keeps the spirit chained by its constant need to be sheltered from harm.

Fear has no place in the light, however, because the very nature of your authentic self *is* your protection from all harm. When working in the light, there is no loss, no failure, no mistakes. When working in the light you intentionally bring in all this wonderful, courageous energy from the universe, and within that sphere there is absolutely nothing to fear. So, dear Lightworker, fear has no place within your spirit. Live your life free from the constraints of failure, because it doesn't exist. Every endeavor is not a chance to succeed or fail, but an opportunity to learn and grow. Fearlessness is pursuing your dreams with a true intention to help others This is what a Light warrior does. Fearlessly.

Honor

Honor your path. As we travel through life we sometimes forget we are on a journey to our creator. As we travel through human experiences we should be purposely moving toward spiritual enlightenment. Illumination and spiritual expansion are why we have come to this life at this time and place. This is a scared path and should be treated as such. What a noble role we have been given! The gift of life and the blessing to learn more and rise higher through the realms of creation is a privilege. Your path is as individual as your fingerprint. It is also what you make of it. You can chose to use this opportunity as a chance to be better or you can dwell in the dark spaces of humanity. No one experiences the pathways the same way, because we have been given the gift of perception. We create our own realities by how we perceive things. We meet and interact with others (in relationships), but each person's path is all his own, and only we can honor the road that brings us to the higher ground. This doesn't mean only honoring the good parts: We must embrace our faith when we hit the bumps in the road as well.

No one ever told us that our journey would be a straight highway off into the horizon. There are twists and turns and potholes along our path and most likely a collision or two. These also must be honored. How we maneuver through the obstacles is what builds us up and strengthens our resolve. Do we get stuck on the side of the road and watch others pass us by? Or do we tap into our spiritual GPS and find our way home? Honoring the inconveniences (because in the big scheme of things, that's all they are) along the way allows us to embark on a restorative journey that constantly expands our light energy. This is being a Light warrior and not a victim of life. This doesn't mean you cannot feel sadness or experience personal pain; it just means that you are embracing your pain and growing from it. No one's path is without these challenges, but without life's hardships we would never experience the joyous times.

Gratitude

Along with love energy, gratitude is the highest emotional vibration you can create. Love and gratitude are the "power couple" of universal energies. Living in the space of constantly being grateful transforms our perspective easily. If your coworker is promoted, don't feel overlooked; feel grateful that you have a job. If your neighbors are able to move into a bigger house in a "better" neighborhood, be happy for them and grateful you have a home. Understand that there are people who would love to have a job or four walls and a roof. It is all relative, and we must express gratitude each day for our blessings.

As we discussed previously, the energy we create attracts more of the same type of energy into our lives. If we consistently generate the energy of being grateful—seeing the glass half full, feeling blessed for what is good in our lives—we immediately begin to shift our focus and magnify the miraculous life we have, thereby calling in even more miracles. We will never again feel victimized by the injustices of life or be disappointed that we don't have what our neighbors have. We will feel blessed and inspired to be better because of what we *do* have. A Light warrior feels blessed with each day she walks the earth, and seeks to share this blessing with others.

Balance

The universe of the energy can be very polarizing. To every high there is a low, to every joy there is a sorrow, and so on. The universal energy exists on a continuum from light to dark and everything in between. When a Lightworker polarizes her energy she is thrown out of balance. Lightworkers who are not balanced in their energy will quickly become drained of their light, and with this comes a lot of unpleasant side effects. Depression, addiction, dysfunctional relationships, all are symptoms of a Lightworker who has become polarized in her energy.

It is easy to polarize in your relationships. Their native sensitivity and empathy cause Lightworkers to overextend their light energy, thus creating a situation that is very easily polarized by both parties involved in the relationship. Each interaction must be balanced with an equal energy exchange. Think about the way we use currencies: We give something to get something. This is similar to an energy exchange. We give something to get something, and everyone is made whole. When we are not made whole in relationships, and one takes more than the other, Lightworkers quickly polarize into the darker spectrum of universal energy, which is, as I mentioned, very difficult to claw your way out of. So keeping mindful of staying balanced and grounded in your energy will help keep you on the middle ground.

The human love experience can at times become an addicting emotional roller coaster of polarization. You can actually become addicted to the soap opera–like dramatizations of your relationships. Many times a circular pattern of "break up to make up" will develop, and your human side will become attached to the highs and lows, the agonies and the ecstasies. This quickly becomes tiresome and throws us into a dangerous cycle of dysfunction that ultimately places the Lightworker in the victim role. The Light warrior, on the other hand stays balanced and knows when his light energy is being depleted by his partner. He does not revel in the drama of dysfunction; in fact he finds it boring and a waste of his precious energy. A Light warrior has much more important things to do! He will give his love generously but also love equitably, which is the only way to create healthy bonds and stability in relationships. It's all about balance.

Practice

All of the techniques to end to the victim role will be of absolutely no use to you if you do not make a conscious, daily effort to practice them. The warrior traits are inherently yours; they are already deep within you, but may have become buried under wounds of the ego-driven human fears. But this fearless warrior is waiting to emerge. Healing your wounds, clearing your energy channels (chakras), and habitually engaging in a positive internal dialogue is a good start to your practice.

Lightworkers sometimes get so caught up in the issues of others that they forget to take care of themselves. You may feel like you're being selfish if you take time for you or assert yourself. When you feel that people have overstepped your boundaries, it is healthy to define your limitations. Healthy for you *and* for them. When others around you put expectations on you to take responsibility for their wounds or to fix everything for them, they are clearly asking you to do the work for them. A Lightworker who even attempts this is misguided. Just as you worked through your spiritual pain, others must do so as well. A Lightworker is meant to guide others out of the darkness, not personally take on the pain of those they are assisting. You must differentiate yourself from others' pain. This is a challenge for so many Lightworkers, who at times can feel the weight of the world's pain on their shoulders. Remind yourself that you cannot heal the world by yourself, but that you can be part of a powerful collective of Light warriors.

How do you maintain this clarity in your Lightworker role when personal connections cloud your judgments? A good start is keeping a tight harness on your gifts and knowing the difference between healing and enabling a loved one. Also, ask for clarity. Each day set aside a few moments for yourself and ask your higher sources for insight on this, because when human emotions come into play, clarity can go out the window. We can easily lose sight of what our role is (or should be) when interacting with loved ones, and sometimes we need divine assistance to find clarity once again. There is no more comforting place to go for guidance than the higher realms.

During meditation you will raise your vibration to a level that is able to receive help and guidance from teachers and guides from your place of origin. This is a very important spiritual practice for a Lightworker, because it keeps you open to a pure dialogue with the divine. By practicing these techniques and incorporating the Light warrior traits into your life, you will never assume the victim role in a relationship again.

The Shift

When the healing shift occurs, you will feel like a bird out of a cage. Free from all the emotional baggage of your past relationships, you can feel safe to love freely again. As a Light warrior you will see a marked difference in all your relationships, because you are now engaging from a power position. In the past, without realizing it, you were taking a part in the dysfunction of your relationships by allowing yourself to fall into the victim role. Now, as a Light warrior, you will have a chance to reboot and begin again. The attributes you bring to the table in relationships will be used to create lasting and healthy bonds. You may find preexisting relationships improve, heal, and even flourish. You may also find that relationships that are not for your greatest good will come to an end. However it won't be painful to let go, because you will no longer feel the human imperatives of fear and validation attached to this person. You will love him or her unconditionally while knowing that it is best to part ways. Things will certainly change for the better as you kindly and gently assert yourself with your loved ones. By abandoning the victim role you will find that you will expand your light energy naturally and achieve mastery of your Lightworker role.

PART V

CHAPTER 16

Escaping Our Comfort Zone

N ow that you have done all the internal work, opened your heart, and readied yourself to love again, what is the next step? Where do you begin? First ask yourself where you feel most comfortable. How have you become complacent, to the point of feeling empty and alone? Do you want to shift out of this comfort zone? Lightworkers often feel isolated and separated from the rest of humanity. So they find safety zones and settle in there, away from all the confusion, stress, and sadness of the planet. The truth is that our sensitivities make us different, but we are still a part of humanity. We may not always fit in, exactly, but that is only because we came here to make the world a different place. Being different does not necessarily mean segregation or isolation; it simply means that your presence brings about transformation. After years of pain, it's only natural to want to seek shelter. When you become aware and achieve mastery of your role, however, you can learn how to handle the constant bombardment of energies and emotions. If you feel stuck in a rut or trapped in a comfort zone, this indicates it's time to push out of your protective comfort zones and get back into relationships and healthy bonding with others.

Feeling safe and in control of your own energy is important. Many Lightworkers who have disconnected take companionship solely in their pets (as we discussed previously); they may even develop hoarding or other unhealthy isolating behaviors that force them into isolation because others simply cannot deal with them. Letting go of these behaviors can be unsettling and frightening. Why should you bring down your protective shield? Why not just stay in your own little world where you are safe? Know that these types of behaviors give you a false sense of security. Although you may think you are protecting your energy, without human interaction, your energy becomes as stagnant as a muddy pond. This causes you more harm than simply going out and taking in all the energies, allowing them to flow through your spiritual body, and learning from the love experiences. It's really about discovering *new* comfort zones that are actually good for you. Remember: You are in a healing process, a journey that takes place one step at a time.

How to Break Free

So how do we let go of the protective behaviors that isolate us? There has to be a desire to love again and step out into the light. The authentic desire should be calling to you. Once the heart chakra is open it will be your guiding voice. Lightworkers may hear their heart calling but not know where to begin. Being closed off for so long, they may feel that opening up is an insurmountable task. Life is about living, and staying complacent in a life that is not fulfilling is not why you're here. You will know when it is time to step out and begin breaking free of your confining comfort zones. After all your healing and internal work, and when you feel the pull to try to step out again, your natural inclination will be to connect with people through love. Once you are cleared and open, your heart chakra will hunger for healthy light energy. Relating to others as both a healer and a human being will become part of your journey once again.

Let go of the past

Painful experiences from our past linger in our consciousness and create anxiety that we will be wounded again. Living in the present is key. As we discussed, sometimes it is hard to let go of the past,

but as you work through your pain it should get easier. The present time is safe. The pain is in the past
and the future is uncertain, so keeping in the present will help you feel protected as you begin to ven-
ture out. Do not worry about what has happened or
what could happen; that is all a part of your journey.
What is going to come will come. Decide to make it
a wonderful adventure without fear. Keep in mind
that today is a new day, a new beginning. Hold tight
to the ultimate truth that your pain is in the past and
your best days are still ahead of you.

Clean out your closet

Many times it helps to throw things out, both
literally and figuratively. It sounds simple to throw
out an old Valentine's Day card, but for some
Lightworkers this represents a letting go of pain,
and they find it very difficult. If you feel this way,
try this exercise.

Meditation Exercise

✦ Get into a comfortable position and begin
   to relax into a meditative state. As you ease
   into this state, set an intention to reach your
   higher self, the one that is in touch with your
   energy. Allow the human ego to go to sleep.

✦ Envision a closet. Let it appear in any way
   that seems natural. Is it a walk-in closet, a
   pantry, a sliding double-door closet? This
   will be your energetic closet.

+ Open it up and begin to look around. What do you see? Is it cluttered? Are there items that look useless or broken?

+ Begin to look through and pick up each item you find. As you examine each item, ask yourself if it is useful to you in this time in your life. If you feel it is needed, put it back where you found it. If it is a useless item, discard it by offering it up to the universe. Envision it being whisked from your closet and evaporating into a white light up into the air.

+ When you feel you have had enough, stop the exercise and gently return to the physical world. Releasing too much at once is not helpful. Remember: This is a process.

If you feel so inclined, clean out your physical closet, as well. As you discard unneeded or useless items, identify where they came from and what they represent to you. Each item you discard, either literally or figuratively, should have a history behind it. You will find you may be attaching emotional value or memories to random items that no longer serve you. Release them and make room for new memories.

Learn to trust again

Stepping out of your protective shell requires the courage to trust again. Because you have been taken advantage of or wounded in the past, you may find it difficult to trust others with your emotions.

A Lightworker who loses her faith in humanity is like a bird in a cage. You are virtually trapped in a cage of your own pain. Remember that the universe is full of love and support and good people. Getting back to your authentic self, the part of you that recognized the good in the world and sees the silver lining, will help support this understanding. Remember that the pain that was inflicted on you is a reflection of the pain the inflictor. We all live with pain that must constantly be processed and healed. Otherwise, people usually deflect their pain onto others. So try not to take it personally, because the ones who left you in pain are in pain, too. Trust that there are people who are in alignment with your authentic self, the you who is now healed and ready to love. Trusting that people are inherently good will help you attract people with good intentions.

Let go of expectations of perfection

The human experience is not one of perfection; it is trial and error. It is about gathering knowledge and growing through experience. Unrealistic expectations of perfection will send you back into your shell before you even get out of the gate. All the enlightenment and spiritual progress in this lifetime will come from the imperfect human experience. Expect that things will go awry at times, and welcome the challenges that come. Let's face it: Perfection is not all it's cracked up to be! In fact, life is not designed to be perfect. As well, the need for perfection shows a need to control. If you are always trying to set things up so nothing can possibly go wrong, you're overextending yourself and creating unnecessary anxiety. Perfection is a place reached when you find happiness and support in relationships. Yes, things will go wrong; it should be expected and dealt with as issues arise. Don't worry about everything being perfectly aligned, or your relationships will always fall short of your expectations.

Push your boundaries a little at a time

When you begin to step out of your comfort zone, it is important not to overdo it. Pushing your comfort level just slightly past your limit a little at a time will help keep anxiety to a minimum. It's not the best idea to jump into the deep end of the pool—outside your comfort zone—without a life vest on. Start in the shallow end and slowly ease into the deep end as you learn to stay afloat. Each time you feel vulnerable or at risk of being emotionally harmed, use your intuition to move a little further from your comfort zone. When you see you are safe, you will be inspired to keeping moving farther out.

Keeping your safe place in your line of vision is also a good idea. For example, if you feel you need to assert yourself with others, there's no need to go on an all-out aggressive rant; that wouldn't be your way, anyway. Start with a calm and loving dialogue explaining your needs. This takes you a little past your comfort zone and your habit of not honoring your own needs in a way that minimizes anxiety and confrontation. With each little step you will find yourself farther away from the wounded person you once were, the one who was closed off to others. If you feel afraid to meet new friends, begin slowly by seeking out people like yourself. Common interest groups or support groups are safe places for you to begin to take those small steps in reconnecting with others. A pen pal or internet forum is another safe place to start, but they shouldn't take the place of real-life, in-person interactions.

Switch up your daily routine

They say complacency is the enemy of success. When we become complacent and don't challenge ourselves, we have nothing to gain. We settle for a mediocre job or unsatisfying relationship because we are so accustomed to it or want don't want to risk making a change. This is a dead end that will yield the same results that caused you to close off in the first place. If you typically sit at home every Saturday evening, maybe it's time to get out. If your routine is sleep, work, home, and back to sleep, maybe it's time to incorporate some new, fun activities. If you have had the same circle of friends for many years and you do not feel honored in these friendships, maybe it is time to switch things up and seek a new circle of friends to add to your life. Change is good; it helps you grow and nurtures your capability to adapt. Switch up your daily routine to take you outside your comfort zone and see what wonderful new opportunities await you!

Let intuition be your guide

Intuition is one of a Lightworker's most powerful gifts. Use this gift to help you break free from of your fears and find healthy relationships. If you take a chance, trust yourself and push the boundaries of your comfort zone. Remember: You have nothing to fear—you have backup! You will know when something just doesn't feel right. This is how intuition works. If you finally feel ready to reengage and are fully open to meeting someone new, but something feels amiss, this is your powerful intuition telling you that this relationship is not for your highest good. Intuition will tell you this relationship is in opposition to what is right for you. Intuition always has your best interests at heart and will be your greatest ally and safety net. Follow its powerful lead, and it will never steer you wrong. If you follow your intuition and embody all the Light warrior traits we discussed, you will have the courage to walk away if it is for the greatest good.

Stay open to possibilities

Last on our list to stepping out of your comfort zone is to stay open. Do not close yourself off from others because you feel it is too far gone or too late. It is never too late for you to find the love of your life, never too late to make a new friend, and never too late to mend a relationship. Yes, you may have fumbled the ball in the past, and you may have lost your faith in love, but you need to believe that your best days are yet to come. A person is never too old or too late in the game to mend fences with loved ones. If you are estranged from a family member or friend, you can reunite with them with a new perspective. You now have clarity regarding what role you can take on in relationships without being taken for granted or hurt. If you feel you're done with someone, it is not too late to heal your pain and forgive him or her before moving on. Anything is possible. Strengthen your sense of belief and have the courage believe in love again. After you do all your healing work, things will shift, and your relationships will reflect the internal changes you have made.

These are only a few suggestions to help you to step out of your comfort zone and into the light again. You will find your own way, and what works for you as you go through trial and error in breaking out of your comfort zone may not work for others. Remember that comfort zones by their very nature are restrictive, and a Lightworker gets to this place because of fear. Lightworkers don't do their best work staying comfortable. Lightworkers are bold and always moving forward. Stagnation and isolation are the two single worst situations for you to be in. So when you find complacency set in, and you know you're ready to move on, do so slowly and with a plan. What makes you a bit uncomfortable now may end up being what puts you in the place

to meet the love of your life or heal a cherished relationship that has been damaged by misuse of your
energy. It's a new day!

CHAPTER 17

Setting Healthy Boundaries

ightworkers love to help and heal, and this is a good thing. However there are times when a Lightworker will base his own self-worth on his success (or lack thereof) in helping others. This is unfortunate because it creates a disastrous cycle of unhappiness in personal relationships. When some people get the idea that you are available to help without limitations, they will take advantage of this. They will begin to cross the healthy boundaries of personal connections.

Lightworkers are often inclined to take personal responsibility for the pain or unhappiness of others. I have observed that when a Lightworker is personally involved, he often lacks the clarity to separate himself from the other person's pain. This makes the sensitive Lightworker inclined to engage in codependent relationships or be the target of those who seek to manipulate him or hold him hostage to his own need to help. Walking away from these needy manipulators feels fundamentally wrong to a Lightworker because it goes against his life purpose. In this sense empathy can become an overwhelming negative dynamic in a relationship.

It is not wrong or selfish to set healthy boundaries. When you learn to address your own needs first, you will begin to understand this. These healthy boundaries must belong to you; they are for you to follow, not for others to heed. We all control our own path and journey. To put boundaries on someone else would be surrendering your power again. As well, to expect someone to never cross your boundaries is an unfair expectation. Setting healthy boundaries for yourself is empowering and gives you full control of what you will and will not engage in, in terms of your relationships.

Remember we have discussed balance and separating your human needs from your spiritual healing needs. When others continuously overstep your boundaries, you will feel used, abused, and taken advantage of. This is the purpose of taking ownership of your own boundaries.

Begin With You

Take a look back at the history of your relationships. What patterns have become repetitive themes in your love life? Do you find you attract people with deep internal pain or addictions, or who are emotionally unavailable, or have honesty issues? If so, you are leading with your spiritual healer identity and not your humanity. When connecting with others, honor your own humanity and its needs as well as your spiritual needs. There is a balance you can create by setting personal boundaries without feeling guilty or neglectful of your true spiritual nature. If you seek a loving, satisfying relationship, you must seek to fulfill your human needs first. So healthy boundaries really mean that we must toe the line ourselves if we expect others to honor us.

For example, if your partner has a spending addiction and it is destroying you financially, how do you set boundaries to protect yourself? Your first response may be to cut up her credit cards, but how does this create a boundary? Isn't it only a temporary stop-gap measure? The solution goes much deeper then placing the boundaries *on* your partner by cutting off her spending capabilities. This will only enable her and give her the power to secure another way to feed her addiction. It has to go deeper than this. Look inside and ask yourself, *Why am I with a person who is creating my financial ruin? Why would I allow my home, savings, and future to be at risk, all for her addiction? What need am I satisfying by allowing this in my life?* More than likely you will discover that you are seeking to satisfy your own need to fix and make everything all right for everyone around you. Your partner is in pain (clearly displayed as an addiction), so you feel you must also be in pain. Dig deep to find out why you would engage in this codependent relationship and take the steps to fill the void that it is currently filling.

Once you have identified why you would allow this and have worked through it, set your own boundaries in terms of what you expect and do not expect from a life partner. What you are willing to accept and what is a deal-breaker. If your partner will not deal with her issues on a deeper level and continuously creates situations in which you are always practicing damage control, then you are taking part in the destruction of your relationship. Instead ask yourself the tough questions and determine whether your partner is in alignment with you and what you want from a relationship.

Compartmentalize your healing gifts

Drawing the line around your healing nature and compartmentalizing it will put things in proper perspective and appropriate placement in your life. Your healing nature must have boundaries, and you must enforce them—put teeth in them—yourself. This requires a lot of self-control and discipline. You will need to retrain your thought processes and categorize your priorities. A conscious daily awareness is needed to keep up the shifts until they become second nature. You maintained the healer role all these years, and it became a misplaced gift in the context of your personal relationships. When you begin to consciously shift your approach to relationships, a new way of engaging with others will come to light. Remember: You are not abandoning your healer role; it is inborn and will emanate through your very existence no matter what you do. All you will be doing is learning to harness it, protect it, and honor it in its rightful place in your life.

Setting boundaries always begins with you first. Being aware of how you are seeking wounded partners and stopping this process is a really good start. Whenever you notice that you are shifting into the caretaker role, or when you have landed in a codependent relationship, it calls for enforcing your boundaries. Lightworkers will sometimes be unaware of what is happening until, one day, they finally realize they are unhappy. It is never too late to take a step back and reset your boundaries. You have every right to an equal energy exchange in your relationships, and if you feel you have begun to backslide with a loved one, begin to look at the boundaries you have set for yourself and reset them.

Here are some boundaries for your inner healer. Use them as is, or use them as inspiration for your own individual needs.

- ✦ I will reset when I begin to feel that self-validation equates the happiness of others around me.
- ✦ I will reset when I begin to feel responsible for someone's pain.

✦ I will reset when I feel the need to correct someone's mistakes for him.

✦ I will reset when my I see I am enabling someone who has an addiction.

✦ I will reset when I am giving when I shouldn't.

✦ I will reset when I am giving more than I can spare.

✦ I will reset when I begin to feel I am being taken advantage of.

✦ I will reset when I do not feel that my emotions are being honored.

✦ I will reset when I am being blamed for the unhappiness of others.

Again, you can input anything into this reset process that resonates with you. If you feel your personal boundaries are being crossed, hit the reset button! The conclusion is you must set your boundaries, not so much for others to follow, but for you yourself to honor. Just as you are not responsible for the pain of others, others are not responsible for setting your personal boundaries. Just as you cannot heal everyone or those who do not wish to be healed, you cannot enforce boundaries on others if you do not enforce them for yourself. This is all about taking responsibility for how you allow others to treat you. In a sense you teach others how you wish to be treated. By putting your own personal boundaries in place, you empower yourself.

Give yourself permission

One important aspect of setting your own boundaries is knowing that is okay to do it! You have a right to set boundaries. Many times Lightworkers are so selfless and dedicated to their mission that they put aside what they need in order to live a joyous human existence. You can be so concerned for others that you forget you need to be loved and honored in return while you complete your divine mission.

Giving yourself permission to care for yourself and set boundaries is sometimes an issue because of the guilt that sets in all too easily. You will find you want to protect people from being harmed or in pain. You came here as a helper to humanity, so it is only natural to want to help others, but not at the expense of shutting off your healing so completely that you feel a sense of failure. Find peace in the knowing that these boundaries will help you keep your spiritual gifts safe and at their most powerful so you can share as much light energy as possible. This understanding will help you ease those guilty feelings. Knowing that the boundaries will help yourself and others makes them easier to accept. If you do not put them in place, others will only be enabled to hold onto their own dysfunction and pain through your interactions with them.

At times a Lightworker will try so hard to keep everyone happy that she forgets to peer deep inside people. Your partner's behaviors are a reflection of his authentic self. If he is wounded at the core, no sense of superficial happiness will be lasting.

Personalizing his bad behavior is a self-centered way of looking at your partner's actions. In other words, if someone treats you badly, this is a true indication that he is suffering. Abusive or unhealthy behaviors give you a glimpse into what is happening with your partner, energetically speaking. You cannot change your behavior or adjust the outward situation sufficiently to take that pain away. So do not let the human ego allow you to take someone's abuse personally. It is *not* all about you, and it is *not* your pain to heal. This is not to say you should sit back and be abused! This is where you give yourself the permission to draw the line and set your own personal boundaries regarding what you will and will not accept in honor of your journey.

Boundaries may represent a form of tough love for a Lightworker, but the emphasis is always on the love. All limitations on a Lightworker's love stem *from* love. In actuality you are helping the other person heal by letting him process his own pain, rather than carrying it for him. If he doesn't own his pain, he can never release it. So allow others to own their own pain, because although you can assist, you have no right to wrest their personal healing journey from them. Lightworkers almost always have loving intentions, but sometimes they are misguided. Just as you have healed your spiritual wounds to open up to love again, others have to heal themselves, as well. Lightworkers are spiritual guides who lend their energy to others. They do not give it away with nothing in return. As we discussed many times the universe is always in perfect balance, and giving away light energy and never accepting any in return will quickly put a Lightworker in a dark place. Understanding that boundaries are a significant part of your healing gifts gives you permission to set them for yourself.

Take ownership of your boundaries

Now that we understand that we are the ones who set our personal boundaries, how do we lovingly let others know? We do not want to alienate people we care about or shut them out, but to gently keep them in a respectful place when interacting with you. This can be a challenge, especially when people are not used to you asserting yourself this way. Your partner may see it as a rejection or proof that you no longer care. That is okay. He is entitled to his feelings and thoughts. Remember it is never too late to shift your relationship into a healthy one. If both partners really want it to work, they will synergize to make it a success. If your partner doesn't want to engage in synergy and will not accept your new ground rules, this can be an indicator that he is not ready to heal himself. (Remember that by setting personal boundaries for yourself, you are also asking the other person to takes steps to begin his or her own healing journey.)

When discussing your wishes, put the rightful ownership on yourself. Knowing that you are responsible for your own boundaries takes the ownership off others; you can even word it this way to avoid painful reactions. Boundaries should be presented as personal choices, with ownership and empowerment, and send a clear message without being accusatory or confrontational.

Following are some ways (in bold) that people often present boundaries that may not be helpful, followed by the self-empowering way (in italics):

I will no longer allow you to bully me.

versus

I will not allow my partner to bully me.

Son, stop asking me for money to feed your addiction.

versus

I will not enable my son by giving him money when he asks.

My boss needs to stop piling work on me every day.

versus

I will not take on work assigned to me that others should be doing.

Every day on my way to work people cut me off on the freeway, and I become upset.

versus

I will not allow a careless driver to upset my pleasant drive to work.

The statements that begin with "I" empower you to have control over what happens in your life and puts the effort of maintaining boundaries on you. This takes away the victimization and calls in a very powerful control factor in your life. This is how you set healthy boundaries and take responsibility for your own happiness.

These "I' type of boundaries also keep you from putting the full weight of your own happiness on your mate, which is also unfair. This empowers you and shows your loved one that you aren't throwing blame around. Keep in mind you are partly responsible for letting the relationship fall into the codependent or dysfunctional state that it's in. If you take ownership of the part you have played, your partner may follow suit and begin to look at his own role in what went wrong.

Boundaries are a Lightworker's best friend, but they must be empowering and they must begin internally. Once you determine your limits and you incorporate these warrior traits into your life, you will find that most people respond in a positive way. They will respect your strength and may even begin to find healing in their own lives, all because you're not empowering them with enabling behaviors. That's what I call a win-win!

CHAPTER 18

Learning to Give and Receive Equally

Throughout this book we have discussed the importance of balance quite a bit, and how important it is for sensitive, empathic people to stay balanced in their energy flow. As we process the love energy, it should flow in and out uninhibited. This is an art form that some Lightworkers have difficulty mastering. This ability usually comes at the end of your healing journey and discovery of your authentic self, because you must have your heart chakra ready and open to receive the love energy.

After being shut down for a long period of time it may feel a bit unnatural to take in new, healthy love energy. It can feel uncomfortable or even selfish to receive. When you are on a path of giving, receiving may feel inauthentic or foreign to your human side. But your spirit knows it has to take in healthy energy to thrive and grow. There are some helpful practices that can assist you in learning to receive without the pangs of guilt or feeling selfish. So how do you begin to let others into your heart space again? Here are some starting points.

Resist the Empathy Trap

As we have discussed Lightworkers have a powerful sense of empathy. When you're practicing how to give and receive equally, remember to put your inner empath in its rightful place. Empathy has its place in your personal relationships, but it should not overtake your role as someone who can receive love, as well. You will know when you are falling in to the empathy trap when:

+ You feel pulled in many different directions as you are trying to satisfy everyone around you.

+ You feel drained by your relationships instead of their enhancing your life.

+ You feel resentment toward the person or people for whom you feel empathy.

Any number of issues can trigger your inner empath to spring into action. This will just set you up to close off your heart chakra again. So being aware when you are taking on the emotional baggage of others is the key to stopping it before it starts creating toxic energy.

Commit Random Acts of Love

Giving and receiving love are two sides of the same energetic coin. No matter what type of love energy you're talking about (remember the six types we talked about in Chapter 9), it is always a give-and take process. So in order to give, you must receive. Why not initiate the process yourself? What better way to find the path than to take the first steps? Find your comfort level at each step and try not to overreach. Begin small by wishing a stranger good day or holding the door for someone. Even the smallest gesture will start the universal flow of love moving into your life. The energy of the universe is always ebbing and flowing, and what is put out will eventually return to you.

I used to do this little trick that was so much fun. I would take a dollar bill (money is most definitely an energy exchange) and place it in a random place for someone to find. Once I put one in between a pile of job applications at a supermarket. Another time I slipped one into a box of pencils in the school supply section. All of these were random places where people would be pleasantly surprised to find a dollar. The value of the dollar never went so high!

I would put a sticky note on it and write: "May this dollar bring you many blessings; what money cannot buy, love will always provide." I secretly hoped the recipients would pay it forward, but I had no attachment to what they did with the dollar. Although I did not put any expectations on this gesture, each time I did it, within a few days I would receive an unexpected blessing in my life. I gave love and received it back tenfold *every single time.* So this is a good example of giving love first and then sitting back and watching as it miraculously is returned to you by the universe.

Observe unconditional love in all forms of life

When we love without conditions there is no fear—no fear of not measuring up or being good enough, no fear of loss, no fear of rejection. We are truly loved for who we are. You can observe this practice most easily in the ones who do it best, children and animals. Your pets love you even if you're poorly dressed, even if you have gained weight, even if you are in a place where you don't like yourself very much. Your pet will love you without conditions. We have so much to learn from animals. The simplicity and completeness of the way they give of themselves is inspirational. Children are the same way. A child will love an adult who spends time with him or her. Nothing grandiose is needed, maybe reading a book or taking time to observe how a bumble bee pollinates a flower. Children display limitless love that asks for so little in return. Their hearts are truly open and overflowing with love energy. If you watch them closely and mindfully, you can learn so much about love from pets and children.

Be fearless and love without expectations

Yes, you can dare to love without expecting something other than love in return. Our human self likes to attach strings to love. We like to leverage outcomes and evaluate potentials the moment we engage with a new person: *I love this person because he could be my future husband, I love this person because she makes me laugh,* or (one of the best ones I have heard) *I love this man because he is organized.* We can be stubborn and put expectations on old relationships, too: *Someday my ex-husband will change* or *When is my best friend going to get her stuff together?* With these statements come the expectations we set on others. Again we are giving away our power to love and be loved by expecting someone else to change or take action. What if he doesn't turn out to be good husband material? What if he ends up being a slob? You won't love him anymore? What if your friend *never* gets her stuff together? Is this really going to change your feelings? Think about the expectations we put on our friends. Why does the love experience have to have these expectations? Expectations mean you will see results or get something back that is of value to you or that enhances the relationship. But what we are overlooking is that the love energy exchange alone holds the most value. Setting expectations always brings disappointment. So when you practice giving and receiving, don't expect anything tangible back. Just appreciate the energy exchange and anything else that comes of it is icing on the cake.

Manifest your love and enjoy the results

Empaths are wonderfully creative souls. You may think, *Oh I don't have a creative bone in my body.* This is most likely untrue; you just haven't tapped into that empathic part of yourself that holds a love for art, the written word, or music. Creating is always a wonderful way for you to channel your empathic energies. It doesn't matter what you create; find the platform for creation that feels right for you. Even if it means baking and decorating a cake, this could be a wonderful expression of love and creativity. This creative exercise will give you an opportunity to create or manifest something physical out of the love flowing through your heart. Put all the love and energy you need to express into this creation, and watch the feelings of self-love that you can accept from this joyous creation come back to you in return. Remember: All things hold energy, not just living things. This creative endeavor will truly be a labor of love, and you will receive love energy back each time you share it with others, admire it, or reflect on the emotions and feelings that came via its creation.

Push through feelings of vulnerability

Once you have been closed off to love you will always remember the dark place you were in. This will create a fear of trusting others enough to be open to their love. This is precisely when you need to allow yourself to feel vulnerable. No more hiding or shielding yourself. You are already out in the light and you need to have the courage and temerity to remain there.

The way to turn this vulnerability into fearlessness is to shift your perspective. The old adage of *nothing ventured, nothing gained* applies here. If you do not put yourself out for and to others, you will never gain the love that is waiting for you. You can now love exponentially and naturally without the fear of pain because you know where there is love there is no pain, only growth and expansion of your light energy. So do not be afraid of rejection, disappointment, or being hurt. Remember: All situations are put before you to teach you about your true path. Nothing in the universe is random. Feeling vulnerable is not necessarily a negative thing; it just means you are bold enough to risk your emotions in order to learn and grow spiritually. It's about showing the world your authenticity and not hiding anymore behind façades. Think about how freeing that is. What a relief it is to shed your insecurities and show the world who you really are! If you are able to look at your vulnerability as actually being brave enough to take the opportunity to expand your light energy, you have now become a Light warrior. Being vulnerable in this context takes on an entirely new meaning. Take the value from each interaction and use it as a chance to increase the love energy you embody even more.

Don't attempt to win someone's love

When you set out to give and receive love, it should be an organic process. If you feel you need to change your appearance, change the things you enjoy, or change anything about your authentic self to meet the needs of someone else, you are falling into a big trap. Lightworkers by nature want to please and be of service, but they need to remain true to themselves always. If someone does not accept you for who you are, attempting to change for him will eventually backfire. Trying to win someone's love with overly generous acts or gifts will not produce the results you hope for. Love must be a mutually beneficial exchange wherein both parties are on equal ground. Remembe: If you feel you have to change to gain someone's love, this change will never allow him to know and love the authentic you that you worked so hard to nurture. Eventually you will begin to lose sight of this authenticity once again. Anytime you feel you have to prove yourself or take action to make someone love you, the love is fear-based and false, and will eventually end in some kind of wound or damage to the love energy you're channeling. Be brave enough to hold tight to your authentic identity and show it to the world; they will love you for it! People can sense inauthenticity in a heartbeat and will eventually lose interest and tire of the mask you are putting on to placate others.

Surround yourself with positive people

As we go through our daily routine we interact and exchange energy with all kinds of people. As a Lightworker you may actually feel drawn to people with issues or deep-rooted problems, but when you are recovering your love energy you should seek people who have a healthy and positive energy flow. There will come a time and place to help and heal, but in personal relationships, refrain from taking on those whose deep wounds prevent an equal footing in the relationship. So now is the time to seek out new people who give off the same loving, positive vibe you are looking to establish for yourself. When making new friends, make a purpose-driven effort to seek out people who are happy and balanced. When we engage ourselves with positive people who clearly have clarity in their own lives, we take in the energy they are giving out, and it helps us keep our own energy uplifted.

Most importantly, having an awareness of how you are balancing your energy flow is going to help you to manage giving and receiving. Awareness is the greatest gift you can give to yourself. Be mindful of what's going on in your relationships, and correct patterns of energy exchanges when you feel they are not for your greatest good as soon as possible. That love energy needs to flow in and out of your heart chakra like the tide. This will enable you to both give and receive in equal measure.

CHAPTER 19

The Path Back to Love

I am hoping this book has sent you on a journey of healing and self-discovery. The many years you have spent in relationships in which you felt devalued or taken advantage of can be seen in a new light as opportunities to grow and evolve at your very core. It's been said and written before many times, but the path to love really is a path of self-discovery. Healing yourself is quite a humbling journey. Facing your darkest fears, digging up old wounds, and clearing toxic energy takes a lot of courage. Once you have detoxed the love energy you channel, how do you know when you are ready to take on the human love experience again? You will encounter many signs and synchronies that will make the answer quite clear. The universe has a way of bringing opportunities into our life with divine timing and only when we are truly prepared to experience them. The wonderful part is that with your newfound clarity, you will now be able to recognize what the universe will deliver to you on a silver platter.

Miracles Abound

It may sound like a bunch of New Age rhetoric, but it is true that when you reach this new level of awareness, miracles will flow into your life. The true miracle is not so much that the world has changed, or that people have changed, or even that your luck has changed. The real change that creates the miracles is within you. Just like Dorothy in *The Wizard of Oz*, you've had the power inside of you all along. With all the hard work you have done you have changed many things about your energy, which in turn will finally allow to you to use this power. You spent many years trying to help others, but somehow you lost yourself in your healer role. Now the shift back to an authentic life gives you the permission to use your power to have all the good things you deserve. Before this time you never allowed yourself the chance to experience love on such a real level. It's time to get back into the game. Perhaps you have been alone and without a romantic partner for many years, but now that your heart is open again, you feel a stirring. Where do you begin?

Give Up and Surrender

The first way back is to give up trying to control things. Surrender to the divine flow of life and let it all unfold naturally. The simple fact is once you have come to the right space in your energy, love will come looking for you. This is similar to couples who try desperately to conceive with no luck, but when they finally stop trying, they become pregnant. It is the same way with love. When you sit back and wait patiently, good things come via the proper avenues and the proper time frame. It seems that when we take action to *make* things happen, we create this mock setup of what love is supposed to be. It is artificial, not organic. Also when we take deliberate action to find the perfect person, we are usually acting from a place of fear. Fear, as we already know creates desperation, and desperation causes us to make very poor choices, indeed. So the concept of giving up and surrendering doesn't mean throwing in the towel; it means allowing things to occur naturally and having the faith to hand the universe the reins.

This surrender takes courage, patience, and ultimate faith. Keep in mind that the fears may creep in from time to time or may never fully be removed, but you can control the fear of never finding the right person. Throughout all the internal work you have learned to trust your instincts and intuition, and trust that everything that occurs is for a purpose. So during this time of letting go, trust the source who gave you all these wonderful gifts in an endless supply of joy. When you get to a place of real peace with yourself and your past, it really won't take very long for the right person to come into your life, because you are now ready for him or her. The universe has given you all the right stuff—now it is time to maintain your balance, love yourself, and practice trust that love will find you.

This does not mean you are to stay shut in your home and that love will be delivered to you like a pizza (or maybe you're hoping for a good-looking UPS delivery person?). Honestly, giving up and releasing the control doesn't mean standing still and waiting for love to knock on your door. It means continuing to live a satisfying life, content with the way things are, living life on your terms and being true to yourself always. It also means finding a circle of people who are not drawing from your energy all the time, and, most of all, taking time to love yourself. Do the things you love to do, do what you're good at, and interact with all kinds of people without expecting anything in return.

Don't let tech take over

The Internet is an amazing way to connect with and meet people whom we would have otherwise never known existed, from places all over the world. But for now, as you begin to re-engage with others with this new perspective, do not try to find love via the Internet. For anyone who is living in newly discovered authenticity, looking for love online can quickly send them into an illusory, alternative world.

The Internet is filled with all kinds of wonderful people, but it also sets up a scenario of inauthenticity. It can be a place where wounded people shield their energy behind a glass screen. It's the perfect place for the wrong person to say all the right words and convince you that he is someone he's not. Also, in my experience with my Lightworker clients who are on online dating sites, they usually end up finding narcissistic attention addicts. Seems that these types become addicted to the attention they are getting, based on their profile. They constantly cruise for new people to chat with and on whom they can try out their inauthentic online identity. Most times when my clients do finally meet these people in person, there is a vast discrepancy between the created online identity and the real person. Sensitive Lightworkers are quickly drawn in by their wounded energy, and the cycle begins again.

One client I had met "the man of her dreams" online and remained in contact with him for more than a year. She told me how excited she was to be going to the "compound" where he lived and talking to him about how he had achieved all these creative projects that were revered by people all over the world. I warned her that the energy of this person felt out of sync or deceptive to me, but she was so taken in by this man through e-mails and online chats that she insisted she was about to start a new life in a new state with this perfect, creative partner.

After 10 days she returned back home and told me she felt she had to literally run for her life. The man was not what he claimed but was in fact a violent alcoholic. Of course she was devastated and hurt. She felt foolish for wasting year of her life and was traumatized by the entire experience. Of course this is an extreme example, and this is not to say you could never find love on the Internet. Thousands of people do, but when you have just emerged from a healing journey, you have to find the most clearly evidential path to love you can. Smoke and mirrors will only lead you back to a place of darkness and being wounded by people with predatory energy.

Don't neglect the other love energies

When you return to the path to love, it is not all about romantic love. As we already discussed, love has six vibrational levels. Here they are again, briefly:

Sexual or passionate love.

Deep friendship.

Playful love.

Longstanding love with a mate.

Self-love.

Love for humanity.

It is so important to balance yourself by embracing and exercising all six vibratory levels of love energy. This will keep your energy well-rounded and stop you from being hyper-focused on romance (or children, or any other type of vibration). We already discussed polarizing your energy. When you remain focused on one type of love in your life, you will polarize your energy toward only one aspect of the entire love energy. When we focus on only one vibration of love, we do not get to enjoy the fullness of life and of love. It's like trying to figure out a six-piece puzzle with only one piece. It is impossible to make out the entire image clearly. Staying well-rounded in the way you give and receive love (on all levels) helps keep the energy flow balanced. It also keeps you interacting and creating bonds on all different levels. You will see how staying balanced and embracing all six types will actually keep you open to all the love vibrations and make room for the universe to bring them into your life.

Enhance your life on your own

The path back to love also includes enjoying your own company. Again this is not a return to isolation. This means loving yourself enough to be content to sit with yourself and be fully satisfied. Being introspective while taking long walks is a wonderful way to enjoy your own company while staying in touch with your authentic self. Enjoying nature and connecting with the beauty of the earth is another way. This will keep you grounded and centered in your energy, and it really does require some alone time.

Empaths also need to express themselves creatively. Journaling and expressing your thoughts through writing is a wonderful way to release toxic energy. Journaling your thoughts is something you need to do solo. If you find it difficult to write, try another way to create. Many Lightworkers find crafting, drawing, or painting wonderful stress relievers and great way to cleanse the energies that you take in empathically after a long day. Empaths tend to respond visually and aurally, so even listening to music while reflecting on your day will assist you in releasing dark or negative emotions or energies and sorting out issues that challenge you in life.

Meditation

We've already discussed meditation a few times, but it bears repeating that meditation is a very important practice in keeping you in touch with your core. Solitary meditation practices, as opposed to those that are guided or that take place in a group (yoga, for example), take you on your own journey anywhere you wish. This way you have total control of your practice and the manner in which you practice it. Your daily meditation can be a ritual that is a staple in your routine or it can be spontaneous, whenever you feel ungrounded. You should have total control over how you reach a higher state of being by your meditation practice. It is wonderful to partake in a group meditation, where you can all collectively gather and feel the power of each other's energy, but having your own solitary, personal practice that is always accessible to you is imperative.

Have fun!

When you decide it is time to love again, remember that life is fun! Perhaps it's been so long that you've felt happy or complete that you've forgotten that life is an adventure and something to be enjoyed. When you are worried about healing everyone else around you, it's easy to forget to partake in enjoyable activities. The fun element in life was swallowed up in all the seriousness of your Lightworker role. Being a Lightworker doesn't mean you're always waging a deadly serious war on darkness. Life is a gift to be lived and enjoyed. Find something you totally enjoy, just for the fun of it. Do not attach a cause to it or an agenda; just do it because it's unapologetically fun! Release any guilt that may creep up during this time and just enjoy yourself. You have given so much for so long—isn't time for a little fun? Give yourself permission to rediscover the fun in life again.

These are just starting points. Returning to love can be a little unsettling. So when you're reengaging, treat yourself with kindness first and foremost. We all make mistakes, so be forgiving of yourself when you do. You have a divine purpose, but you also have a human life to live out, a life that is meant to be joyous and filled with love. Keeping the love energy flowing begins with yourself. It's also important to realize that the healing path never ends. Once you get to the sacred place of self-love, the only thing to follow is pure magic.

Epilogue

Now that you have embarked on this healing journey, you are securely on the path back to love. Learning to understand the difference between the spiritual love energy and the human love experience and honoring the need to connect on both levels at the same time will allow you to adjust your energetic frequency accordingly. You are now aware of six different types of love energies and why it is important to channel all of them to stay in balance and keep your energy flowing and equitable with others. Most importantly you have discovered that all relationships begin with you. Your balance, your openness, your empathy, your boundaries, your pain, all are beautifully yours to own and embrace. All aspects of your connections with others should be considered sacred gifts from our creator. Each time you embrace your personal power in relationships, you take a step toward growth and stepping into the life you desire. When you heal your pain and open your channel to love, you also become a powerful manifester. You can call in all that is good and healing within the universe, with love as the driving force for all you will ever need. Throughout this book you have walked a humble path back to a healing place where you had the courage to face your pain. Finally the energetic chains are released, and you are free to receive love as you give it.

Honoring the responsibility you have been given to maintain a healthy energy flow (of both giving and receiving) empowers you to prevent others from victimizing you. It also helps prevent you from becoming a victim of your own sensitivities. The whole process back to love is one of empowerment and ownership of every part of the journey. When you maintain a victim identity you continuously victimize yourself because you hand over the responsibility of your own healing journey to others. The challenge here is that no one but you can own your pain and heal your spirit. You must always look internally before you can begin to find love externally.

Hopefully this book has given you some tools to stay the course and remain in that space of empowerment and authenticity. Take time for yourself and stay in touch with your own needs and points of connection with others by continuing development of your conscious awareness. Remember to always love yourself unconditionally. Don't overlook the little things in life that bring you joy, such as a peaceful walk in nature or just watching the sunset. The simple things will help keep you centered and bring you back to your focal point when things become overwhelming. You are a Lightworker and a light warrior. You have a sacred purpose, so never forget to honor your path and the role you have taken on in this lifetime. But above all, always honor yourself.

Index

245

About the Author

Sahvanna Arienta is an internationally known psychic advisor and spiritual counselor. Her work helps others recognize their authentic selves and find purpose in living a heart-centered existence. Her unique style and connection to others are powerful healing tools that have been revolutionary forces for change in the lives of her worldwide clientele. She is the author of *Lightworker* and *The Lightworker's Source*.